Introduction
To Kabbalah

The purpose of this book is to show you how to use **Kabbalah Cards** for raising your level of consciousness to receive higher insight and life-guidance from your inner self. In the process of reading this book and using these cards, you will also be introduced to the **Kabbalah**. If you would like to begin using Kabbalah Cards right away, skip this section and begin reading the one entitled: **The Kabbalah Cards.** Later, when you are more curious about the Kabbalistic tradition behind what you are doing, return to this introduction.

There is a legend that Kabbalah was taught to Adam by angels. He was told that it was to be an eternal wisdom-key which will eventually guide the human race back into *Paradise*. Adam passed it on to his sons, and from that time to the present it has continued to be passed on. Another legend tells us that Moses learned Kabbalah in the temples of ancient Egypt. However, in a different version we learn that he received it when he went to the top of Mt. Sinai. According to this version, Moses felt that Kabbalah was too pure and too powerful to be shared with the general public. He was then given the Ten Commandments for the masses, reserving Kabbalah for those who proved themselves worthy to receive answers to the deeper questions.

Throughout the history of the world there has existed an oral tradition of passing on knowledge. In the earliest times, these teachings included much of what we now consider to be common knowledge. History, math, music, the natural sciences (including health and medicine), customs and religion were all passed on *from mouth to ear.*

There were levels of the oral teaching, the deepest being reserved for the few. This esoteric body of knowledge revealed the core of sacred wisdom. Why was it taught in secret? For one thing, only a few were interested in making the effort necessary to prepare themselves to understand it. Like today, most were content with the level of consciousness described by Isidore Friedman as, "The bed, the belly and running around".

The deeper wisdom cannot be communicated to individuals who are not open to the sacredness of it. Speaking of deeper things to a superficial mind is to talk of color to a blind man who lived his life in a blind society - it is meaningless.

Through the pain of experiencing one disappointment after another, we eventually seek deeper understanding. This is often accompanied by a vague, subtle sense that there exists, has always existed, a body of knowledge about life that can give us the answers we need, and teachers of this knowledge who can help us find *our* way. This search for the sacred takes us on a journey through *ourselves.* Along the way our hearts are opened, then our minds and finally our inner eye. We are ready to *see* the deeper reality behind appearances; we are ready to learn, to tread the way, to receive *The Secret Teaching.*

The Secret Teaching of the Oral Tradition is fundamentally the same in every culture. You will find it in the heart of Christianity, Buddhism, Taoism, Hinduism, Zoroastrianism, the teachings of the Cherokee, Judaism, Ancient Egyptian architecture, Huna, African tribal myth and ritual - it is everywhere. Once you learn even a little bit of it, you will see it glowing in the mystic-fire core of the philosophy of

Plato, in myths and in fairy tales , in nature, in art and science, and especially in the religions of every culture throughout history.

Kabbalah is the Secret Teaching as it was received and passed on by a mystical sect of the Jewish people. The oral tradition of passing on wisdom-secrets has been part of the Jewish culture for as far back as history can take us. In fact, the word Kabbalah translates from the Hebrew to mean, *From Mouth to Ear*, suggesting the whispering of a secret from one individual to another.

The earliest written record of the teachings of Kabbalah was possibly penned in the first century; historians are not clear on this, but most agree that the writing occurred no later than the fifth century. The name of this document is the *Sephir Yetzirah* (Book of Formation) and it was written in a combination of Hebrew and Aramaic.

The following is the final paragraph of the *Sephir Yetzirah*, to give you a feel for its style and content:

> "Abraham bound the spirit of the twenty-two letters upon his tongue and the Tetragrammaton disclosed to him their secrets. God permitted the letters to be immersed in water, He burned them in the fire and imprinted them upon the winds. He distributed them among the seven planets and gave them to the twelve zodiacal signs."

You may go to many Jewish temples today, and you will not hear references to astrology, or Kabbalah. Some Jews regard Kabbalah as archaic, empty superstition. Others praise it as the mystical heart and spiritual core of their religion and their race. Many do not know of Kabbalah's existence, let alone its connection to the Judaic heritage. And yet, today as it has been down the corridors of time, Kabbalah is taught, practiced and whispered about by Jews and non-Jews alike for the food it offers to the spirit that yearns for something more.

It was not until the early part of the Middle Ages that the teachings of Kabbalah were published in detail, and it was around that time that these teachings were named, *Kabbalah*. Writings from many authors of various parts of Europe were gathered together, formed into several volumes and collectively titled, the *Sephir Zohar* (the Book of Splendor).

Here is a brief quote from this massive work:

> "He could not answer him, so they went and asked R. Simeon. He said: 'The Companions have explained that the name *El* (one of the Names of the Divine) indicates sometimes mercy and sometimes severity. If men are virtuous, *El* is there standing for lovingkindness, and if they are not deserving, *El* is there standing for severity and is called *Gevurah*. The real truth, however, is as follows. *El* everywhere stands for the light of Supernal Wisdom which exercises its influence everyday, and without which the world could not stand a day before the heavy chastisements that arise everyday against it.'"

Even these brief views of the *Sephirs Yetzirah* and *Zohar* reveal that the meaning behind these early writings are not easy to fathom. And yet, they offer deep perceptions of universal truth. Over the centuries individuals who seek deeper meaning have found that study and meditation upon the teachings of Kabbalah are helpful for seeing through the veils of life's mysteries and stepping *consciously* into the realms of the Eternal.

Across the fields of time and around the world Kabbalah continues to be studied, tested, analyzed and interpreted. There are many books in many languages which convey the latest versions and insights of Kabbalah, and of the universe as perceived through its teachings. Some of the more well-known and respected contemporary authors on the subject include, Aryeh Kaplan, Gershom Scholem, Z'ev ben Shimon Halevi, William Gray, and Gareth Knight.

One of Kabbalah's principle focuses is on the letters of the Hebrew alphabet. Kabbalah teaches that these letters were not arbitrary creations, but rather, they are magical, archetypal patterns from which the universe has been created.

Each Hebrew letter corresponds with a word and a number. For instance, the first letter of the Hebrew alphabet is Aleph. Its numerical value is 1 and it corresponds with the Hebrew word for ox.

A Kabbalist would look at that letter, its number and word correspondence, and begin to meditate on these for deeper meaning. For example, it makes perfect sense that the first letter corresponds with ox. In the ancient world, the ox pulled the cart or plow, and the first letter of the alphabet draws the rest into existence.

To the Kabbalist, every Hebrew word conveys the string of meanings associated with each of its letters. Every Hebrew word and statement also conveys a number in the sum of the numerical values of each of its letters. By comparing this sum with the number of other words, letters and statements Kabbalists divine the inner meanings of words, letters and numbers. This method of divination is called, *Gematria*. Kabbalists have used it mainly for interpreting the hidden meaning of the Torah. The Torah was considered by the ancient Kabbalists to be the single most important document in existence, the most sacred of all written texts.

Another major focus of the Kabbalah is a simple, fascinating diagram called, *The Tree of Life* (see diagram on page preceding this Introduction). This diagram is a key to life's mysteries. It represents the structure of the universe as a whole and every individual part of it.

The Tree of Life (*Otz Chim*, in Hebrew) is composed of ten Spheres and twenty-two Paths. The ten Spheres represent the ten essential qualities or aspects of the One Power which causes, rules and expresses throughout existence. Each Sphere is assigned a name and number.

The name describes the quality or function which the Sphere represents. For example, that which is represented by Sphere number 2 on the Tree is named, Chockmah, which translates from the Hebrew to mean, Wisdom. It represents, among other things, the Perfect Wisdom which rules creation.

The number assigned to each Sphere indicates both the sequence in creation of what the Sphere represents as well as the order of its power or authority. For example, that which is represented by Sphere number 1 occurs first in the order of creation and has authority over the forces or functions of Spheres 2 through 10. That which is represented by Sphere number 2 occurs second and has authority over the forces represented by Spheres 3 through 10. And so on. The Sphere numbered 10 represents the final stage of creation, the product or result of the nine Spheres above it.

The Spheres are also assigned other correspondences. Chief among these are the following four:

1. a Divine Name
2. an Archangel
3. an order of angels
4. a planet from our solar system
   (including the Sun and Moon)

The Divine Name refers to the Causal Power behind the Sphere. The Archangel refers to the archetypal pattern of that power in creation. The order of angels represents the astral or subconscious forms which receive and convey the archetypal pattern to the physical world and conscious experience. The planet represents the observable forces and activities in nature and our selves.

These four correspondences represent the four essential levels through which the qualities of the Spheres work. The sequence of these correspondences indicates their order of authority over one another. In other words, the Divine Name represents the power of will or intent; the archangel receives that intent and turns it into a pattern of action; the order of angels receives that pattern and turns it into subconscious forms which will determine physical action and conscious conditions; those physical actions and conscious conditions are represented by the planetary correspondence.

There are also correspondences assigned to each of the twenty-two Paths of the Tree. Four primary ones are:

1. the qualities of the two Spheres the Path joins
2. one letter of the Hebrew Alphabet (there are the same number of Paths on the Tree of Life diagram as there are letters in the Hebrew Alphabet)
3. one of the Major Trumps of the Tarot (there are also twenty-two of these)
4. a planet, or Zodiacal sign (there are ten planets and twelve signs = twenty-two)

The twenty-two Paths represent the twenty-two principle stages of your conscious evolution as you progress through life. Your experiences are constantly teaching and transforming you, moving you toward conscious awakening of life's deepest mysteries, and your potential to know all, be all, do all. This growth process is represented by the Paths. It occurs as a result of the ten essential energies of the universe, represented by the ten Spheres on the Tree of Life, as they play upon you.

The Spheres indicate the essential kinds of forces at work

as you pass through the experiences represented by the Paths. The Hebrew letter associated with each Path offers an archetypal key to what the Path represents. The Tarot Image associated with each Path is designed to attune the subconscious for the reception of the deeper meaning it represents. The astrological correspondence represents the observable patterns and activities in life which express the Image's meaning.

Many think of Astrology as a superficial, non-scientific system for making general predictions that should be scoffed at. This view is held only by those who have not seriously studied the subject. Astrology is a language of energy, both cosmic and psychological. As you learn the language and observe the forces it represents you will discover that your understanding of yourself, others and the universe has been deepened, and your ability to intelligently respond to what is happening has been vastly improved.

Most regard the Tarot as a foolish fortune-telling system aimed at taking advantage of the simple minded. However, this is only a mis-use of a sacred system of symbolic images. Tarot's images were designed by masters of wisdom. They present us with visual ideas of higher consciousness, stimulating higher intuitive insight, life-wisdom and devotion to the spiritual path.

The Tree of Life also consists of Three Pillars. These are the the three vertical columns of Spheres. The Pillar on the right contains Spheres 2, 4, and 7. This is called The Male Pillar because the type of forces it represents are outflowing. The Pillar on the left includes Spheres 3, 5, and 8. It is called the Female Pillar because the kinds of forces it represents are inflowing. The Middle Pillar is the Pillar of balance, harmony and union. The Three Pillars represent a fundamental principle of Kabbalistic teachings: every individual is a combination of male and female energy in some sort of balance. The Three Pillars also represent the principle of polarity or the balancing of opposites which operates throughout nature.

When you look at the Tree of Life diagram, you are looking at a representation of the essential pattern of yourself and the universe as understood by the highest level of consciousness achieved by the ancient seers. By studying its meaning, your awareness is taken deeper, into the eternal realities. We are always experiencing these realities; they are the laws and forces at work within us. However, they remain hidden deep in our unconscious until we take the time and trouble to look for them within.

Kabbalah is a kind of map guiding us on our inward search, a representation of the spiritual dimensions, a language of enlightenment.

The Kabbalah Cards

Kabbalah Cards were invented by me in 1987 as a means of analyzing issues *Kabbalisticaly*. They are based on the Kabbalah Tree of Life diagram, which has been used for countless ages as a devise for raising consciousness for expanded insight, guidance and understanding. One can analyze the universe as a whole, an individual, and any specific issue or situation in life in terms of the Tree of Life diagram. This practice is called, **Placing Matters on the Tree**, and it is an essential aspect of Kabbalah.

You will notice that Kabbalah Cards are extremely simple. There is a card for each Sphere and a card for each Path, thirty-two in all. These represent what is referred to in the *Sephir Yetzirah* as, *"The Thirty-Two Mysterious Paths of Wisdom... which are the Foundation of all things."* On each of the ten Sphere cards you will find the name and number of one of the Spheres on the Tree. On each of the twenty-two Path cards you will find the names and numbers of the Spheres the Path joins. The only illustrations are a circle for the Sphere cards and two circles connected by a straight line for the Path cards. If you examine the Path cards closely, you will notice that the angle of the illustration is consistent with the place of the Path on the Tree.

In your set of cards there are three promotional cards. Remove these three and place them on the side. If you like, you can use the reverse side of these promotional cards for the purpose of meditating on the diagram of the Tree. The more you look at the Tree the more familiar you will become with it, and with the wisdom and knowledge it represents.

You will also find three reference cards in your set. One pictures the Tree with the names and numbers of the Spheres. Another pictures the Tree with the numbers only. Another presents a list of the names and numbers of the Spheres. These are included for your reference to the Tree when you are using the cards. Separate these as well from the rest of the deck.

You should now be holding thirty-two cards; ten Sphere cards and twenty-two Path cards. Check this now to be sure that your set of cards is complete. These are the only cards you are to shuffle and draw from when doing a reading.

When you have used these cards often enough you will find that as soon as you look at a card its place on the Tree will flash in your mind. At first, if you are unfamiliar with Kabbalah, it may seem that the cards are almost too simple to work their magic. However, they are not. They work. They somehow affect the subconscious to trigger deeper insight and reliable guidance just the way that they are.

You might find it most fascinating to use the Cards for a while without referring to the Card Meanings offered in this book. Allow them to work directly on your intuition and creative imagination. Follow the guidelines for doing readings presented in the following chapter, but instead of reading the meaning from the book, simply notice what occurs to you within when you look at the card you have drawn. For some of your questions you may not have an instant insight or idea as to what the card is "telling you". If this happens, just let the card sit in your mind. In time, something will occur. Trust the sense of knowing which arises within you.

How to Do a Kabbalah Card Reading

A **Reading** is the term used to represent the act of placing a matter on the Tree for receiving insight or guidance using Kabbalah Cards. Before doing a Reading, remove the three promotional cards and three reference cards from the deck. Count the cards that remain to make certain that you have all thirty-two Kabbalah Cards in your hand: ten Sphere Cards and twenty-two Path Cards.

The first and simplest Reading is called, A **One-Card Spread**. To do this, ask for guidance or insight regarding any specific issue or for your life in general. Then, shuffle the deck a few times. When you feel that the cards are well-mixed, cut the deck into three piles. Gather those into a single pile any way that you like. Then, fan the deck in your hand or on a flat surface. Give yourself a moment to assume the attitude that your choice is being guided by the Higher Self or Higher Mind within you. Then, choose the card that chooses you, or simply select one at random.

When you have selected your card, turn it over and find its place on the Tree of Life Diagram. You can refer to the diagram in this book, or use the diagram on one of the reference cards you put aside before shuffling. Give yourself some time to permit what is on the card and its place on the Tree to suggest the insight or guidance you need. If you have drawn a Sphere Card, focus on its name and number. If the card you have chosen happens to be a Path Card, focus on the names of the two Spheres the Path joins and allow those to suggest your answer.

If the card itself and its place on the Tree does not suggest an answer to you, or if you want additional insight, turn to the table of contents of this book and find the section heading: **Card Meanings**. Under this heading, look for the sub-section with the title that matches the card you have drawn. Find the page number of that sub-section and then turn to the appropriate page and begin reading.

As you read, permit your mind to freely associate with what you are reading as it relates with your specific issue or general question. You will soon realize the connection, the special message, that the card you have drawn suggests to you at this time. Trust your inner flash of knowing; that is how the Tree reveals all things.

It is not necessary to read the entire Card Meaning for every question. Your answer may occur to you sooner. Stop reading when you feel satisfied. There may be parts of the Card Meaning that seem to fit for you, while others do not. Accept that which does and disregard the rest.

In each Card Meaning you will find a section with the heading: **Kabbalistic Correspondences.** This is included primarily for those more serious or advanced students of the Kabbalah. If it makes no sense to you at this point, you may choose to read it anyway, taking it in as seeds which some part of your mind may respond to. It may be fun to allow your imagination to freely associate with these correspondences. For instance, you might imagine the angels standing before you, giving you some kind of sign or speaking to you in some other way, offering guidance on the issue in question. It is not necessary to believe in angels, to know anything about Astrology, nor to have any familiarity with the Tarot for Kabbalah Cards to work for you.

As far as the Tarot is concerned, its images are associated with the Path Card Meanings. There are no Tarot pictures in this book. The images are described verbally. This is in keeping with the original way that the images of Tarot were conveyed from teacher to student; that is, *orally*. Like the Kabbalah, Tarot was not set down in physical form until the Middle Ages. The descriptions of these images are kept as simple as possible in order to convey the most basic aspects of the image's meaning. Consider these to be designed for the beginner to Tarot Wisdom. As you read the descriptions, build the image in your mind. If that is difficult at first, make your best effort. Each time you make the attempt you will find the image building a little more, until at last it stands in your mind complete, alive and glowing with the wisdom of the ages, and its special hints for the issue under your consideration.

If after referring the the Card Meaning you do not receive a satisfactory answer to your question, the answer you need may require more time to arise into your awareness. Let the Kabbalah Card you drew sit in the back of your mind as you go about the affairs of your day, meditate for a while or go to sleep. Every so often, remind yourself of your question and the Card you drew in response to it. You will receive your inner flash.

If you are not experienced with apparently random systems of divination such as the type described above, a brief explanation may be in order. Random systems based on sacred symbols have been used throughout time, by every culture, as a means of tapping a level of consciousness that is beyond the normal range. This has been the special practice of kings and rulers, as a guide for preserving their position of authority, and to lead their people for peace, prosperity, and victory. Unlike many of the other systems of its kind, Kabbalah divination has not been used by the elite in government or politics, but rather by the elite in wisdom. It is the tool of the sage, not the warrior-king.

Random systems of divination work. Why they work is not all that important, because whether you can explain it in a satisfactory way or not, they do work. Here is one explanation that you may find plausible.

When you allow yourself to select a card because it "feels right" or randomly, you are, in effect, surrendering the selection process to a Higher Mind, with faith in its guidance. This suggests to your subconscious that something deeper, higher, more accurate and profound is going to be revealed. It is the nature of the subconscious to believe whatever is suggested to it, and to respond accordingly. Through a random selection process of this kind, your subconscious is directed to link your conscious mind with a higher level via the card that is drawn; and that is exactly what it does.

Additional Readings

The Ten-Card Spread

"Examine all things by means of the ten Sephiroth."
from: *The Sephir Yetzirah*

The **Ten-Card Spread** is a more detailed way to receive *Tree-Guidance*. For this type of reading, follow the same procedure as in the **One-Card Reading**. However, instead of selecting just one card, this time select ten.

Select them one at a time. As you choose each one, keep it face down and build the Tree of Life pattern on a flat surface. Place the first card you select in the position of **Sphere 1**. Place the second card in the position of **Sphere 2**. Place the third card in the position of **Sphere 3**. And so on. Follow the sequence of Spheres until you have placed the tenth card in the place of **Sphere 10**. When you are done, your face-down cards should match the design of the Spheres in the Tree of Life pattern.

The Card in the first place represents cause; ruling influence; the destined trend that is futile to resist.

The Card in the second place represents the wise approach; what to do about what is happening; growth, change and movement.

The Card in the third place represents what to learn, find out about or explore further; restraints and limitations; areas of ignorance.

The Card in the fourth place represents how and where

A Diagram of the Ten-Card Layout Design

Cause, Comic Will, Deeper Purpose

3rd Position
Lessons to Learn
(Female Influence)

2nd Position
Wise Approach
(Male Influence)

5th Position
Losses

Spiritual Level

4th Position
Gains

6th Position
Love, Balance, Relationships

8th Position
Honors
Intellect
Appearances

Psychological Level

7th Position
Accomplishments
Feelings
Goals

9th Position
Influences from the Past, Supportive Elements

10th Position
Physical Level
Consequences
Rewards
Results

Note: Disregard the description of the levels in the triangles if considering them makes the Reading too difficult. They are included for the more advanced Reader.

to apply Mercy, ease, forgiveness; gains.

The Card in the fifth place represents how and where to apply reduction, elimination, sacrifice, severity; costs and losses.

The Card in the sixth place represents relationships and the way to bring about love, beauty, harmony and balance.

The Card in the seventh place represents feelings, desire, emotion, goals, accomplishments.

The Card in the eighth place represents thought, speech, integrity, self-esteem, and form.

The Card in the ninth place represents influences from the past; memories and imagination; possibly illusions; what you can count on or depend upon for support or what is supporting or upholding the situation.

The Card in the tenth place indicates the way the situation is expressing itself at this time; also, the physical aspects of the situation and what to do on a physical level (physical actions to take).

You will notice that there are more than one possible meanings for each place. It is up to you to choose the ones that fit for you in response to your question.

Optional: The Daath Card. You can add an eleventh card to your ten-card layout. This is called **The Daath Card.** The word "Daath" is Hebrew for, *Knowledge*. It is the name of a phantom Sphere on the Tree. You will see its place on the Tree on the following page. Kabbalists teach that this Sphere is not really there; it is the shadow of the sixth Sphere, where it was placed before Divine Spirit descended into physical manifestation. *Daath* represents our bridge across the abyss of ignorance, the secret path of our return to our Spiritual Source. Therefore, if you like, draw an eleventh card and let it indicate guidance for how to advance in your Spiritual Growth Process.

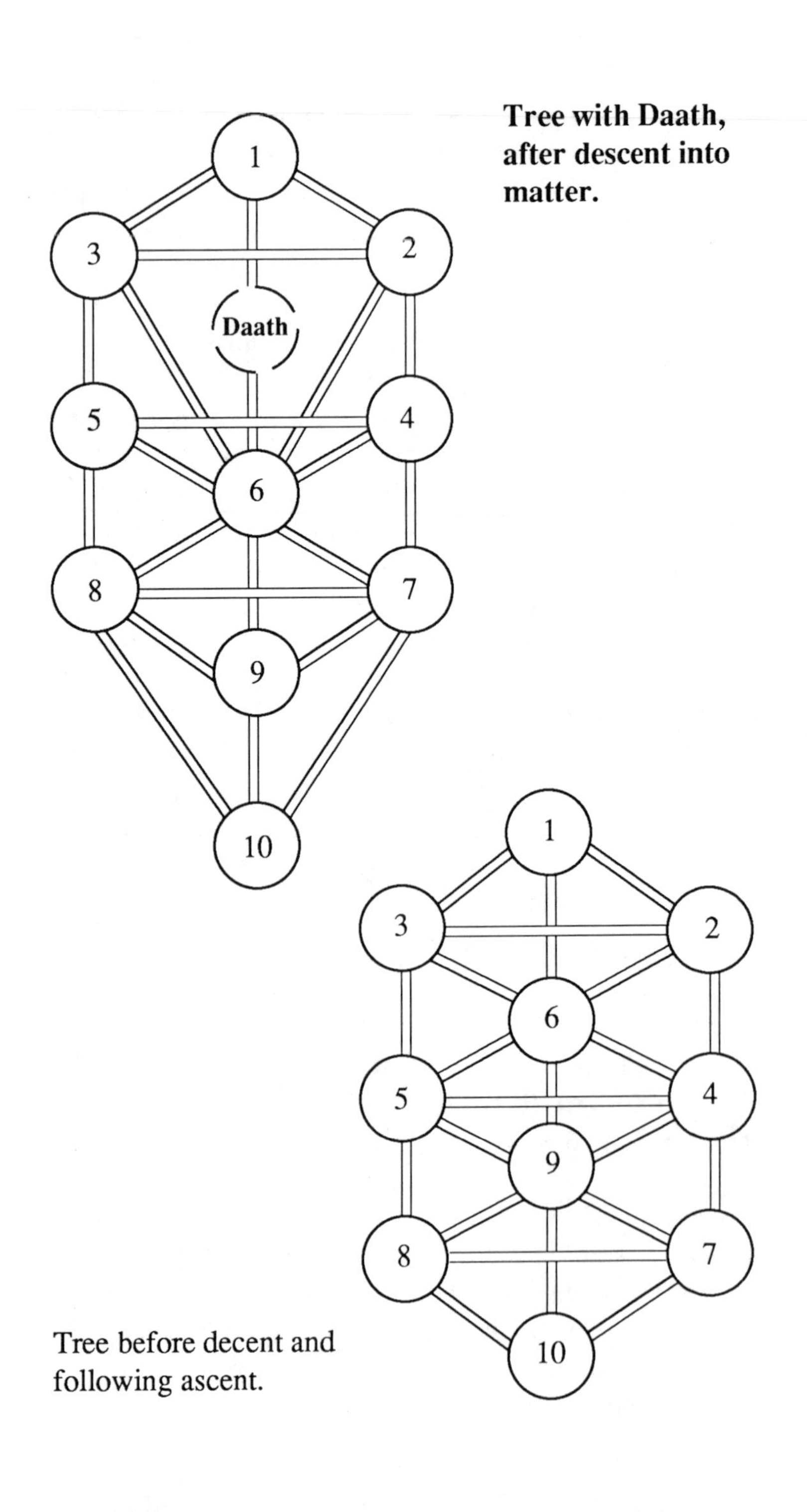

Tree with Daath, after descent into matter.

Tree before decent and following ascent.

When your Tree pattern is laid out, turn the cards over. Examine them anyway that you like. You can begin at the top and work your way down, or wherever you find your attention drawn.

Here is an example. John wanted insight into his relationship with his girlfriend, Kimberly. He did a Ten-Card spread. In the seventh position (the place of Sphere 7) he drew the card **Sphere 1: Crown.** He immediately thought about his goal and desire, which was to marry Kim. Sphere 1, however, suggested to him that the destiny at work is out of his hands. He decided to redirect the focus of his goal. Instead of hoping that she would marry him, he focused on his sense of trust that whatever is best for them both will occur.

Interestingly, Kimberly actually brought up the subject of marriage to him shortly after the reading. She said that she noticed a change in him which she greatly appreciated. Before, she had been feeling a subtle sense of pressure from him, an underlying intensity coming from him pushing her for more commitment. This had disturbed her and made her confused about her feelings. Now that the pressure was gone she was clear that she loved him. She trusted him to respect her freedom to think for herself.

Probabilities

Another application of the **One-Card Reading** is for probabilities. Simply ask your question on a one-to-ten scale, such as, "What is the likelihood that my house will sell this winter?" Then, draw a card and look specifically at the numbers. The closer to ten, the more probable; the closer to one, the less likely. If you draw a Path Card, it means that the likelihood is less precise at this time; for instance, Path 6 to 9 suggests a sixty - ninety percent chance.

Kabbalah Life-Readings

A Kabbalah Life-Reading uses the **One-Card Reading** method to explore several areas. These are:

Spiritual Growth
Health
Finances
Career
Relationship

Simply draw one card for each area to gain insight into your over-all life direction. Shuffle the deck before each question, and ask simply: "Please give me guidance or insight for my ... (Spiritual Growth, Health, etc.)". When you have interpreted it, place that card back in the deck. Shuffle, cut, and draw one card for the next question. Continue this procedure until you have drawn a card for each issue.

Past Life Readings

Kabbalah teaches reincarnation. The purpose of each life is to perfect ourselves as far as possible, until we have fulfilled our potential for growth on earth. Then, we do not have to come back, but rather move into "some better place". For insight into a past life-time, use the same procedure as the One-Card Spread, asking the question: "Please give me insight into a past life experience that would be helpful for me to know at this time." When interpreting your answer, allow your imagination to flow freely. Notice any scenes it shows you in connection with the card meaning.

Goal Manifestation and Spiritual Growth

This is another application of the **One-Card Reading**. Bring a specific goal to mind and ask "Please give me guidance or insight into the best way for me to proceed for this goal." You might try drawing one card for the same goal every morning, and follow the guidance of the card drawn in the way that seems appropriate. Do this everyday until the goal is achieved.

The same method works as a kind of daily compass for Spiritual Growth. Ask the question: "What do I need to know or focus upon for my advancement in the Spiritual Growth?" Do this daily, or as guide for a given period of meditation.

Card Meanings

"Ten Sephiroth and twenty-two letters
are the Foundation of all things"

from: The Sephir Yetzirah

TABLE 1

The Spheres and Their Correspondences

English Title	Hebrew	Divine Name	Archangel	Angels	Astrology	Intelligence
1 Crown	Kether	Eheieh	Metatron	Chaioth ha Qadesh	Neptune	Admirable
2 Wisdom	Chokmah	Jehova	Ratziel	Auphanim	Uranus	Illuminating
3 Under-standing	Binah	Jehova Elohim	Tzaphkiel	Aralim	Saturn	Sanctifying
4 Mercy	Chessed	El	Tzadkiel	Chasmalim	Jupiter	Cohesive
5 Severity	Gevurah	Elohim Gibor	Khamael	Seraphim	Mars	Radical

TABLE 1 (continued)

The Spheres and Their Correspondences (continued)

English Title	Hebrew Title	Divine Name	Archangel	Angels	Astrology	Intelligence
6 Beauty	Tiphareth	Eloah Va Daath	Michael	Malachim	Sun	Mediating
7 Victory	Netzach	Jehova Tzabaoth	Haniel	Elohim	Venus	Occult
8 Honor	Hod	Elohim Tzabaoth	Raphiel	Beni Elohim	Mercury	Perfecting
9 Foundation	Yesod	Saddai el Chai	Gabriel	Ashim	Moon	Purifying
10 Kingdom	Malkuth	Adonai Malak	Sandalphon	Cherubim	4 Elements Earth	Resplendent

TABLE 2

The Paths and Their Correspondences

English Title	Hebrew Letter	English Name	Meaning	Tarot Key	Astrology	Intelligence
1-2 Crown to Wisdom	א	Aleph	Ox	Fool	Uranus	Fiery
1-3 Crown to Understanding	ב	Beth	House	Magician	Mercury	Transparent
1-6 Crown to Understanding	ג	Gimel	Camel	High Priestess	Moon	Uniting
2-3 Wisdom to Understanding	ד	Daleth	Door	Empress	Venus	Luminous
2-6 Wisdom to Beauty	ה	Heh	Window	Emperor	Aries	Constituting

TABLE 2 (continued)

The Paths and Their Correspondences (Continued)

English Title	Hebrew Letter	English Name	Meaning	Tarot Key	Astrology	Intelligence
2-4 Wisdom to Mercy	ו	Vau	Nail	Hierophant	Taurus	Triumphant and Eternal
3-6 Understanding to Beauty	ז	Zain	Sword	Lovers	Gemini	Disposing
3-5 Understanding to Severity	ח	Cheth	Fence	Chariot	Cancer	House of Hidden Influence
4-5 Mercy to Severity	ט	Teth	Serpent	Strength	Leo	Secret of All Spiritual Activities
4-6 Mercy to Beauty	י	Yod	Hand	Hermit	Virgo	Will

TABLE 2 (continued)

The Paths and Their Correspondences (Continued)

English Title	Hebrew Letter	English Name	Meaning	Tarot Key	Astrology	Intelligence
4-7 Mercy to Victory	כ	Kaph	Grasping Hand	Wheel of Fortune	Jupiter	Rewarding
5-6 Severity to Beauty	ל	Lamed	Ox-Goad	Justice	Libra	Faithful
5-8 Severity to Honor	מ	Mem	Water	Hanged Man	Neptune	Stable
6-7 Beauty to Victory	נ	Nun	Fish	Death	Scorpio	Imaginative
6-9 Beauty to Foundation	ס	Samech	Prop	Temperance	Sagittarius	Probation
6-8 Beauty to Honor	ע	Ayin	Eye	Devil	Capricorn	Renewing

TABLE 2 (continued)

The Paths and Their Correspondences (Continued)

English Title	Hebrew Letter	English Name	Meaning	Tarot Key	Astrology	Intelligence
7-8 Victory to Honor	פ	Pe	Mouth	Tower	Mars	Exciting
7-9 Victory to Foundation	צ	Tzaddi	Fishhook	Star	Aquarius	Natural
7-10 Victory to Kingdom	ק	Qoph	Back of Head	Moon	Pisces	Corporeal
8-9 Honor to Foundation	ר	Resh	Front of Head	Sun	Sun	Collective
8-10 Honor to Kingdom	ש	Shin	Tooth	Judgement	Pluto	Perpetual
9-10 Foundation to Kingdom	ת	Tav	Signature	World	Saturn	Administrative

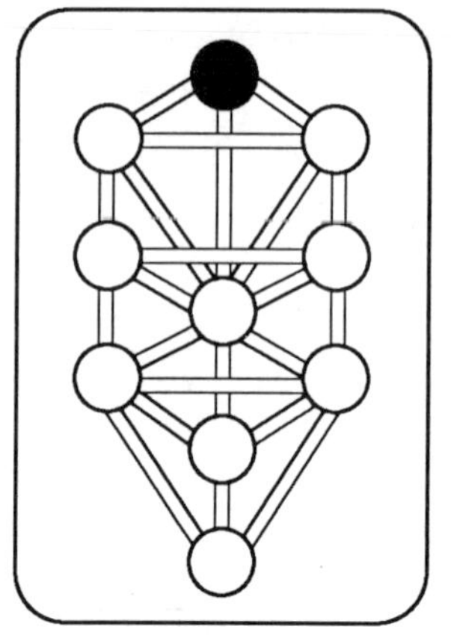

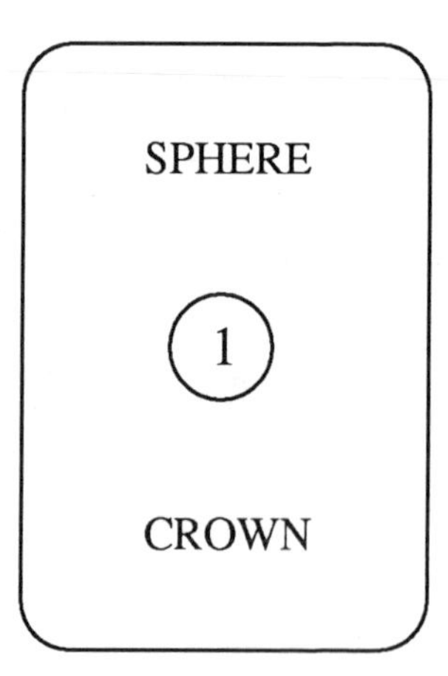

Hebrew Title: *Kether*

Guidance of the Sphere

Trust in a Higher Power of Higher Intelligence taking charge. When your own wisdom cannot show you what is best to do, it is wise to trust that whatever you do will work out in line with your needs. The rational mind can always criticize by focusing on negative possibilities. However, the truth of the matter is beyond its scope.

Kabbalists teach that the center of the center of existence is an eternal mystery. Our experiences and ourselves are essentially unknowable. Resist the urge to jump to convenient conclusions. Opinions block the light of truth as much as they contain it. Learn how to accept the ambiguities and uncertainties of life. These do not necessarily indicate a weak mind, but rather a deeper, clearer more realistic attitude.

Acknowledge your spiritual urge. Kabbalah teaches that the deepest and truest urge in each of our beings is the urge to unite with the Infinite Power. This urge is nurtured, and the Power made more clear and near through the concentration of your attention upon it. Meditation practices, religious rituals and other forms of centering techniques have been passed on for ages as means to this end.

There are decisions in life which are too large to be made. The facts we need are simply unknown. If you have been working at making a decision without making progress, you may have arrived at such a point. Life will have to make this decision for you, or you will make it when you accept that either way it will be made on faith, not facts. You may never know what to choose or which is best. In the meantime, avoid the exhausting strain of indecision by accepting that in the end it is up to you to make the best of whatever happens.

Experience Represented by the Sphere

This Sphere represents the Power of Will which is the cause behind creation. It is pure, infinite Potential. This Power is so great that it is beyond the limits of consciousness to contain. Yet, it is the most sacred aim to seek its awareness of it. It has been referred to as, *That which is beyond name and form, The Causes of Causes, The Primal Will.* Conditions and individuals represented by this Sphere are characterized by willfulness, mystery, spirituality, higher intelligence, concealed authority and hidden trends or intentions that seem to be in control. There may also be a sense of disorientation, for the energy of the *Primal Will* is undifferentiated, meaning that it takes us beyond individuality, and stems from the point where All is One. The experience represented by this Path is teaching you to trust in a Higher Power of Higher Intelligence at work in circumstances that you can neither control nor comprehend.

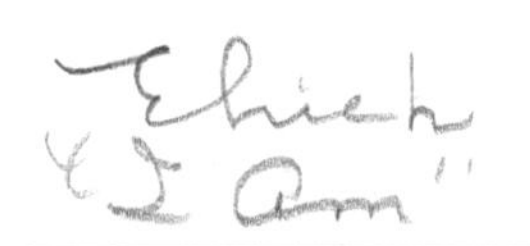

Kabbalistic Correspondences

(use for your further insight and meditation)

The Divine Name associated with this Sphere is, *Eheieh* (pronounced: Eh-heh-yeh). It translates from the Hebrew to mean, *I Am*, suggesting *The Power To Be* or *the power which is beyond name and form.*

The Archangel associated with this Sphere is, *Metatron.* His name is Greek, and means, *Near Thy Throne.* Metatron represents the pattern of will which aligns us with *the highest purpose of being.*

The Angels associated with this Sphere are named the *Chaioth ha Qadesh.* Their name means, *The Holy Living Creatures.* They represent the thoughts and feelings which guide you along the path of True Purpose and enable you to experience the sense of closeness with your Inner Source.

The Astrological Correspondence with this Sphere is the planet *Neptune.* Kabbalists associate Neptune with the experiences of intuition, spiritual vision and religious urges.

The Type of Intelligence associated with this Sphere is called, *Admirable,* because no living being can attain the purity of perfect knowledge which it represents.

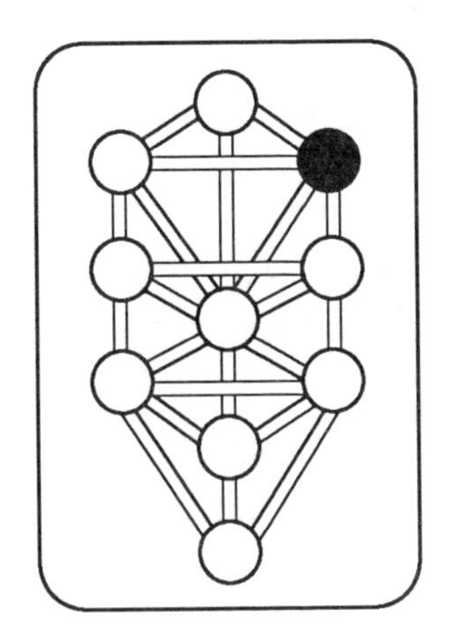

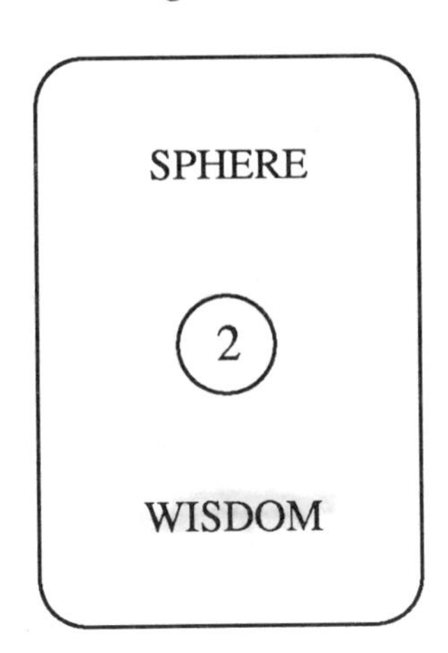

Hebrew Title: *Chockmah* (pronounced: Chok-mah)

Guidance of the Sphere

Apply action that is aligned with your goals. Activity of any kind - physical, emotional or mental - is creative. It stimulates growth and change and gets things moving in the direction of the intent that is behind it. Every action attracts consequences. These are instructive if one is Wise enough to relate with them that way. Remain aware of what is happening in the present and observe the consequences of your actions every step of the way. This will enable to you make adjustments, and to avoid drifting off-course.

Pay attention to what you are doing and how you are doing it. This will reveal more direct and efficient ways to proceed. Keep your goal in mind to help you to act and react in line with it and to keep things moving in its directon. When you are in doubt as to what to do, remember your purpose or objective and hold it in mind; this will soon stimulate ideas of what you can do for it.

Monitor the effects of the force you are using so that you can keep it under your conscious and intelligent control. It is generally wise to avoid extremes of any kind. Caution and moderation are the gateways to wisdom and sound judgement. Wisdom is available to those willing to receive it. Whatever your problem or challenge, keep your mind open to receiving the inner guidance you need. If you fill your head with the sorry belief that you do not or cannot know what to do, you block the guiding light you seek.

Experience Represented by the Sphere

This Sphere represents the pure, masculine energy of the universe, your power to change and grow. Its name suggests the use of wise judgement, and its place atop the Male Pillar of the Tree indicates the Kabbalist's respect for the authoritative nature of Wisdom. *Wisdom is the intelligent application of power.* The color associated with this Sphere is gray, suggesting gray hair, which symbolizes wisdom gained through experience over time. The conditions and individuals represented by this Sphere are characterized by knowledge, prudence, energy, activity, growth and change. Experiences represented by this Sphere are teaching you the laws of life, higher purposes and goals, and intelligent ways of applying force.

Kabbalistic Correspondences

(use for your further insight and meditation)

The Divine Name associated with this Sphere is, *Jehovah.* This name is spelled with four Hebrew letters: *YodHehVauHeh.* It is reverently referred to by the term, *Tetragrammaton*, which is a Greek word meaning, *The Name.* This name is rarely if ever pronounced aloud by those who know it because of the intensity of the stimulating force released by its utterance.

The Archangel associated with this Sphere is, *Archangel Ratziel.* His name means, *One sent forth.* Ratziel represents the pattern of will which directs our actions and forces in line with the most profound purpose of our being. He is said to be the source of Kabbalah, and the custodian of the secret wisdom teachings that enable the human race to fulfill its purpose and potential.

The Angels associated with this Sphere are named *The Auphanim.* Their name means, *Wheels. They* guide us along Wisdom's Path, and attract to us the conditions which are best for our growth. As wheels make it easier to travel upon the earth, the Auphanim make it easier for us to travel through life.

The Astrological Correspondence with this Sphere is the planet *Uranus*. Kabbalists associate Uranus with revolution, sudden change, the distant past and the future. Uranus is also associated with genius and the quick flash of intuition.

The Type of Intelligence associated with this Sphere is called, *Illuminating* because Wisdom is an inner light that guides us.

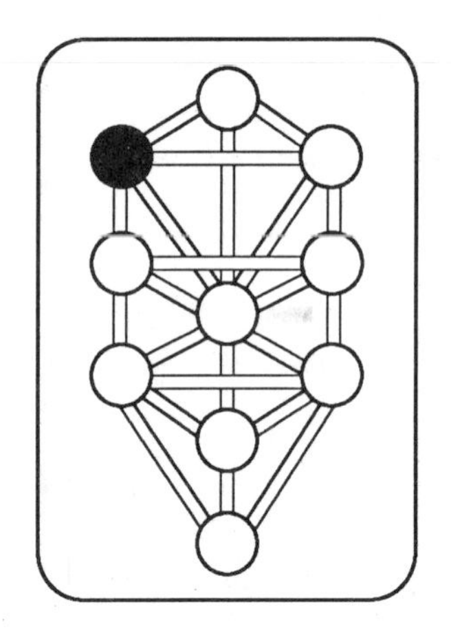

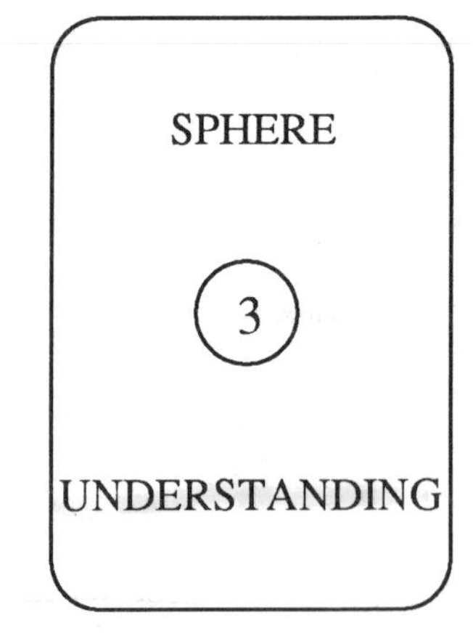

Hebrew Title: *Binah* (pronounced: Bee-nah)

Guidance of the Sphere

Be receptive to the knowledge and guidance that you need. Before you can help yourself or others you must first see clearly what is needed. Draw upon what you know and seek the facts of the present. In this way you can more effectively nagivate through what is happening.

Find out what is going on before taking action to change or direct the situation. Instead of worrying or guessing at what others are feeling and thinking, try asking questions and listening to the answers you receive. Do not overburdon yourself with expecting to know more than you do. Life is a school and every choice is an experiement. Learn from your choices and move on.

Shine a light in the darkness; use your power of understanding to help yourself and others. Explore, examine, research, study and learn. Learning is being forced upon you by your limitations and constraints. Wherever you are and whatever you are going through you can always learn how to cope, how to deal with what is going on in ways that bring improvement. Kabbalists regard your ability to learn or understand as your highest receptive power for it gradually takes you beyond all limitations.

Experience Represented by the Sphere

This Sphere represents the forces of containment, boundaries and limitations which seem to constrict upon us as we grow. It is named, *Understanding* because our boudaries and restraints force us to seek a deeper understanding of what is going on. As we open ourselves to receive it, Understanding blooms within like a flower of peace and illumination to heal our wounds and make sense of our lives. Individuals and conditions representd by this Sphere are characterized by receptivity and restraint, exposure of areas of ignorance and an opportunity for learning. Experiences represented by this Sphere are teaching you your boundaries and limitations and how to patiently stay within them until the times are ripe for intelligent expansion or liberation.

Kabbalistic Correspondences
(use for your further insight and meditation)

The Divine Name associated with this Sphere is, *Jehova Elohim.* It means, *God the Lord* and represents the Power to restrain, contain and conceive of all.

The Archangel associated with this Sphere is, *Archangel Tzaphkiel.* His name means, *Beholder of God.* Tzaphkiel keeps us within our necessary boundaries and reveals to us all we need to know.

The Angels associated with this Sphere are named, *The Aralim*. Their name means, *Thrones*. They help us to find our way and know what to do.

The Astrological Correspondance with this Sphere is the planet *Saturn*. Kabbalists associate Saturn with the experiences of restraint, discipline and patience. Saturn is also called, *The Great Teacher*. He has earned this title because he teaches us our boundaries by imposing sorrowful consequences as soon as we overstep them.

The Type of Intelligence associated with this Sphere is called, *Sanctifying*. This is because Kabbalists are taught to revere their restraints, sorrows and limitation as guidelines imposed by the Perfect Understanding of Divine Will; they believe that what we cannot have, do or know this time is a form of protection, keeping us where it is best for you to be for now.

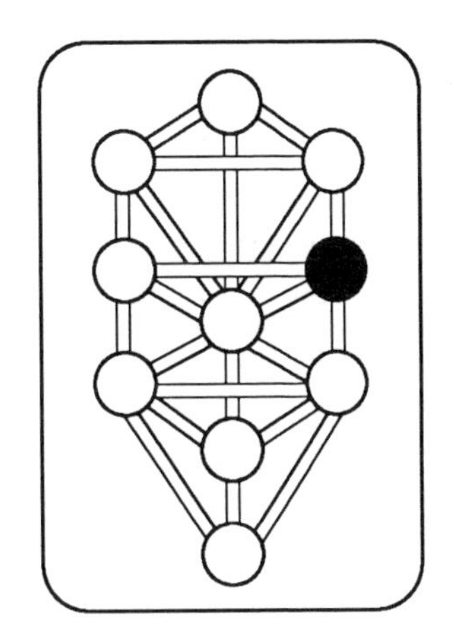

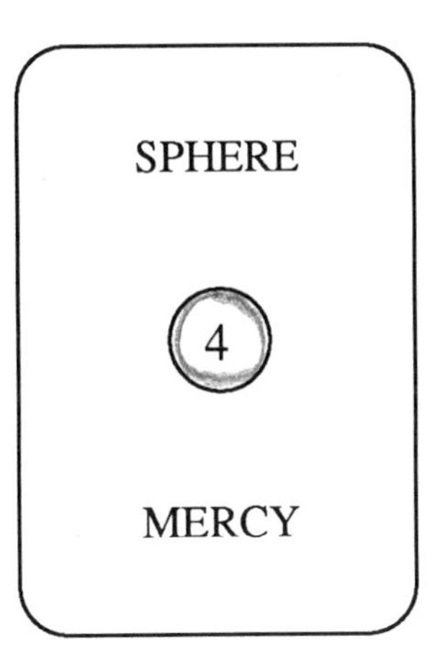

Hebrew Title: *Chessed* (pronounced: Cheh-sed)

Guidance of the Sphere

Identify useful, constructive trends and build upon them. Make use of the resources available and more will be there when you need it. When you have taken full advantage of the opportunities that you have a new opportunity will present itself to take you farther. If it seems that there is no purpose or nothing to be gained by your current situation, you are overlooking the opportunities and advantages that exist Avoid making too much of the problems, difficulties and dangers that you face. That which you focus attention on will seem to grow larger. Emotional reactions inspire exaggeration. It is possible to hold a small coin so close to the eye that it blocks out the Sun.

If you want to empower the forces that are working with you, overlook the trends moving against you. Involve yourself instead in constructive activity that is aimed at your goals. Do not deny the dangers, but do not dwell on them. Focus on what you want to grow. Concentrate on what is working and find ways to take these constructive trends farther. There are bound to be disappointments and set-backs in any significant project or journey. Keep your attention unstuck from negative, critical attitudes and continue moving forward; in this way the building-process has the best chance of overcoming the destructive trends and influences.

Experience Represented by the Sphere

The fourth Sphere represents the processes of expansion and construction. Wherever you look, you can find something beneficial growing, building, expanding. This is why Kabbalists refer to this Sphere as *Mercy*. The fourth Sphere also represents the True Will or Archetypal Pattern of the Self which is growing or expanding through every experience that you have. We experience the Mercy of the universe when we follow this Pattern and take joy in the growth and unfoldment of our True Self. Conditions and individuals represented by this Sphere are characterized by a sense of freedom, abundance, optimism, and opportunity. The Experiences represented by this Sphere are teaching you to focus on positive trends to keep them going, and to involve yourself in a constructive process to continue moving forward.

Kabbalistic Correspondences
(use for your further insight and meditation)

The Divine Name associated with this Sphere is, *El.* This name simply means, *God.* In association with Mercy, it suggests, *Merciful God, God the Giver, God the Creator*. *El* also refers to the Divine Nature of your True Self. It represents the Power to build, to create and to forgive *All.*

The Archangel associated with this Sphere is, *Archangel Tzadkiel* (pronounced: Tzahd-kee-el). His name means, *Righteousness of God.* He enables us to use our forces, resources, advantages and opportunities *Rightly*, so that they will continue to increase, and so that we will not have to pay the price of loss for misusing them.

The Angels associated with this Sphere are named *The Chasmalim* (pronounced: Chahss-mah-leem). Their name means, *Bright Shining Ones.* They represent the hopeful thoughts and feelings you have which help you to carry on. If you persistently look for reasons to be hopeful, *The Chasmalin* will help you to find them.

The Astrological Correspondence with this Sphere is the planet *Jupiter*. Kabbalists associate Jupiter with the experiences of expansion, generosity, joviality and optimism. Jupiter is also called, *The Great Benefic*, because the generous, optimistic attitude that is associated with Jupiter has a tendency to attract opportunity, win influence and exhibit what the common man calls, "luck".

The Type of Intelligence associated with this Sphere is called, *Cohesive* because constructive processes build and expand by including or bringing together more and more elements into a cohesive pattern.

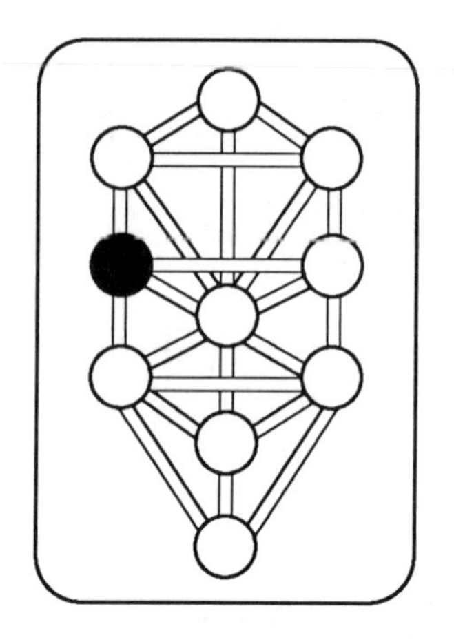

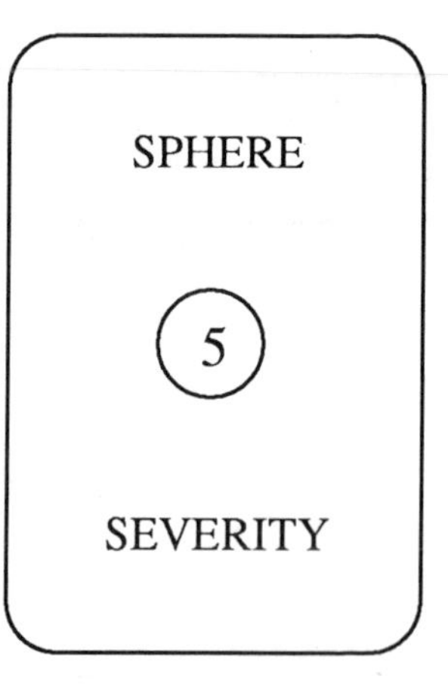

Hebrew Title: *Gevurah* (pronounced: Geh-voor-ah)
Additional English Titles: *Justice, Wrath*

Guidance of the Sphere

In an old, out-of-print manuscript, written by an unknown sage, it is written, "When more severe or radical measures are in order, a passive, flexible approach invites continued deterioration."

Elsewhere in this same manuscript occurs this teaching: "Loss and sacrifice are part of life. Each of us is learning to rise above every necessary loss because the losses do not end until we have realized that no loss can take anything away from our True Self. Every cosmic force, including the forces of creation and destruction, exists to assist the True Self in serving its True Purpose and rising to the heights of its Glorious Potential."

Destruction and loss are as necessary as construction and gain for success in any endeavor. We must have the strength to undo, or do without, the old to make space for the new. We must have the strength to endure the sacrifices that are necessary and to eliminate trends of waste, excess and deviation from your purpose. As in the pruning process in plants, the removal of inferior elements stimulates fresh growth and gives rise to new life.

When it seems that you can do nothing to ward off adversity, focus on eliminating ways that you are making the process more difficult or destructive than it needs to be. When suffering is upon you, examine your past to uncover any unbalanced actions which may have brought you to this point. Do not do this for the purpose of blaming or condemning, but rather do it to help you to make better choices in the future.

However painful or difficult things may seem during cycles of *Severity*, strengthen yourself with the knowledge that a cycle of release, gain and growth will inevitably follow to restore balance at a higher level.

Experience Represented by the Sphere

The fifth Sphere represents the forces of destruction, elimination, reduction and decrease. These forces balance the expanding, constructive processes represented by the fourth Sphere. Everything has its cost. Kabbalists refer to this Sphere as, *Justice*, because they are taught to have faith that every experience of loss, pain and sacrifice is justified and serves a worthwhile purpose. It is also referred to as the Sphere of *Wrath*, because overstepping our boundaries sooner or later attracts some kind of cosmic fury aimed at eliminating the patterns which took us off course. The conditions and individuals represented by this Path will tend to be radical, militant, exacting and, perhaps, *expensive* in some sense. Experiences represented by this Sphere are teaching you how to utilize, overcome and rise above loss.

Kabbalistic Correspondences

(use for your further insight and meditation)

The Divine Name associated with this Sphere is *Elohim Gibor*. His name means, *Lord of Battles*. In association with this Sphere, the name can also be understood to refer to, *God the Destroyer*. This Name represents the Power to win battles, overcome loss, apply discipline and make necessary sacrifices.

The Archangel associated with this Sphere is *Archangel Khamael* (pronounced: Kah-mah-el). His name means, *Burner of God.* Kabbalists associate Khamael with the fiery force of *Zeal.* When one's zeal is strong enough, one is willing to make any sacrifice necessary for that for which one desires.

The Angels associated with this Sphere are named *The Seraphim*. Their name means, *Fiery Serpents*. They give the sly thoughts and feelings which guide you to win battles and to turn apparent defeats into real victories.

The Astrological Correspondence with this Sphere is the planet *Mars*. Named after the Greek God of War, Kabbalists associate Mars with swift, decisive action and courage.

The Type of Intelligence associated with this Sphere is called, *Radical*, because the forces it represents remove trends of deviation and return conditions to their originally intended course.

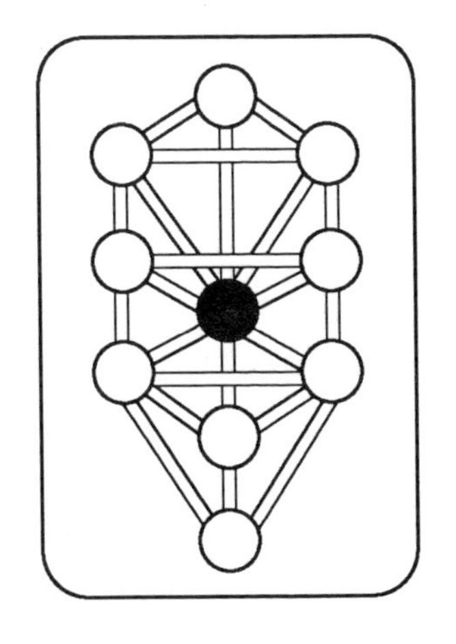

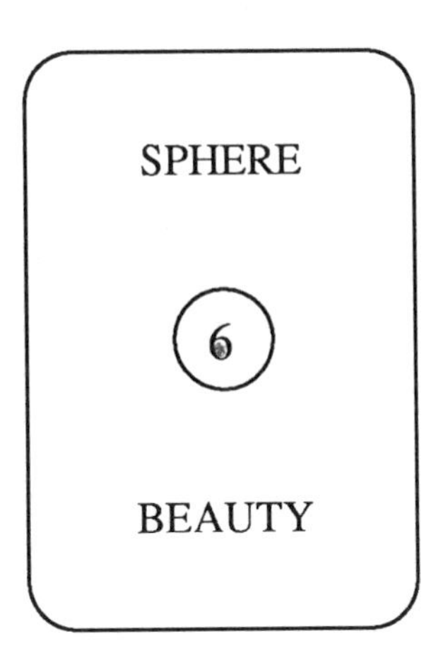

Hebrew Title: *Tiphareth* (pronounced: Tiff-ah-reth)

Guidance of the Sphere

When one is in a position of influence, there exists the opportunity to bring the higher and lower together toward a point of balance and peace. Dedicate yourself to serving a higher purpose. Maintain your balance, harmonize with your environment and and be loving. This brings order and inspires trust and openness.

Love is an attractive, binding force. When individuals work together in harmony all are benefited. Seek others with whom you can join in harmony for your mutual advantage.

Before moving forward, view the matter facing you as a whole so that your efforts do not merely improve one area at the cost of another. Follow the path of balance and love and the universe will support your endeavors.

Look in your heart for the guidance you seek. It is guiding you along the path of balance, harmony and compassion. It is guiding you to *give*. What it suggests that you do may not seem reasonable at first. However, its guidance is beyond the scope of intellect and desire, and it points the way to growth and peace. If you go against its guidance and overrule compassion, the individuals and consequences you attract will seem empty and degrading.

Experience Represented by the Sphere

The sixth Sphere is named, *Beauty*, but it is also referred as, *The Mediating Intelligence.* This is because the force it represents has to do relationships and bringing parts together into a balanced, harmonious whole. It also represents the *Light of Divine Love* which rules the universe. This Love shines from what is called, *The Spiritual Sun,* which illumines *The Light of Truth* within each soul, guiding the individual along *The Path of True Purpose.* It is the *Light of the Logos*, your *Reason for Being*, and it shines within *You.* Conditions and individuals represented by this Sphere tend to be characterized by a powerful binding influence; their interests are more concerned with giving than taking, and they convey a sense of deeper purpose. Experiences represented by this Sphere are teaching you to become less identified with selfish interests, and to follow the urge to serve, to create and to give which guides you from the depths of your heart.

Kabbalistic Correspondences

(use for your further insight and meditation)

The Divine Name associated with this Sphere is, *Eloah Va Daath* (pronounced: Eh-low-ah-vah-dah-ath). This name means, *The Knowledge of God.* It represents the Power to organize, order and arrange all things.

The Archangel associated with this Sphere is, *Archangel Michael.* His name means, *Like unto God.* He represents the pattern of will which guides us on the path of our True Purpose.

The Angels associated with this Sphere are named, *The Malachim* (pronounced: Mah-lah-chim). Their name means, *Kings.* They represent the thoughts and feelings of a loving, balancing, ordering nature, which help you to rise above any problem or difficulty so you can intelligently direct your circumstances.

The Astrological Correspondence with this Sphere is the *Sun* of our solar system because the Sun is the central ordering point around which the rest of the solar system revolves. Kabbalists teach that the physical rays of the Sun carry the guidance and influence of the True Light of the Spiritual Sun, which guides you from your heart along your True Path through life.

The Type of Intelligence associated with this Sphere is called, *Mediating,* for reasons already described.

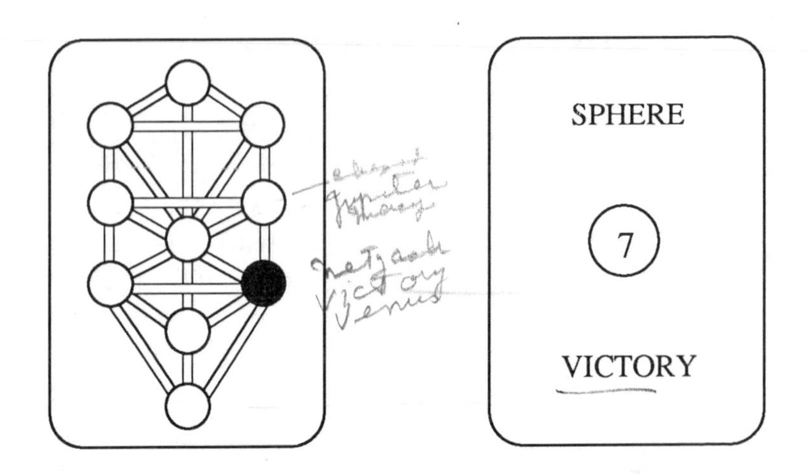

Hebrew Title: *Netzach* (pronounced: Net-zach)

Guidance of the Sphere

Be confident and move toward your goals boldly. This releases your higher potential and attracts opportunity.

Follow your *feelings*. They can *sense* what is happening beneath the surface and *know* what is beyond the rational mind. However, when one is emotionally unbalanced feelings cannot be trusted; they will tend to convince you of what you want to believe or fear is true.

Your feelings are magnetic. They are attracting to you circumstances of like pattern and vibration. As the ancients knew well, we tend to experience what we have faith will happen to us. Feelings draw to you the thoughts you think. Low moods of fear and discouragement attract thoughts which make the worst seem real. Choose your feelings consciously and detach from those which are working against you.

When one is low in vitality it is easier to think negatively. Faith requires *life-force*. A negative view of things can require nothing more than rest, relaxation or some other form of rejuvenation to help you see things in a more balanced and realistic way. Participating in the beauty of romance, art, music or nature can do wonders for increasing one's vitality, harmonizing one's feelings and renewing one's attitude.

Cultivate constructive desires. If you lack interest or motivation to do something that is necessary, you have probably been focused on desires for other things. Take control of your attention and hold it focused on what needs to be done. Drop thoughts which leave you feeling negative or discouraged.

Experience Represented by the Sphere

The seventh Sphere represents the feeling-nature of the personality. This includes the feelings of emotion, desire, romance, the sexual urge and the drive to create art or beauty. It is named Victory to demonstrate the significant influence that our feelings have on ourselves, others and our environment. When one's drives and desires are aligned with achieving an objective, one's success or *Victory* is sure to follow. Individuals and conditions represented by this Sphere will tend to be characterized by creativity, vitality and emotionalism. They are likely to exhibit desirable, empowering and attractive qualities. Experiences represented by this Sphere are teaching you to trust your inner feelings as a guide, and to be self-confident.

Kabbalistic Correspondences
(use for your further insight and meditation)

The Divine Name associated with this Sphere is, *Jehovah Tzabaoth* (pronounced: Jehovah Tzah-bah-oth). This Name means, *God of Hosts.* He represents the creative Power in nature. The ancients imagined *Jehovah Tzabaoth* as the Divine Commander of vasts armies of angels which He would send out to aid and support those motivated by worthy aims.

The Archangel associated with this Sphere is *Archangel Haniel* (pronounced: Hah-nee-el). His name means, *Grace of God.* He empowers us with the drive, vitality and sensitivity to create and appreciate beauty.

The Angels associated with this Sphere are named, The *Elohim*. Their name means, *Gods*. They give us the thoughts and feelings which motivate us to grow toward our Divine Potential.

The Astrological Correspondence with this Sphere is the planet *Venus.* named after the Goddess of Love, Kabbalists associate Venus with art, creativity, physical love and beauty, romantic attraction and harmony.

The Type of Intelligence associated with this Sphere is called, *Occult*. The term *occult* simply means hidden or concealed. It is associated with the Sphere of feelings because feelings can sense things on a deeper level than thought or appearances can reveal.

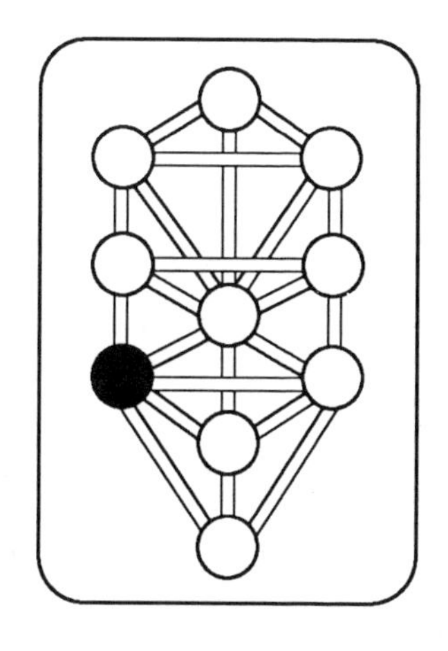

Hebrew Title: *Hod*
Alternate English Titles: *Splendor, Glory*

Guidance of the Sphere

An intellectual approach raises one above the emotional level, where more primitive patterns of reaction may cause disturbance. The effort to carefully, clearly articulate your thoughts, feelings, plans, decisions and observations has a cooling effect on the emotions and brings clarity.

Pay attention to matters of form and appearance. Refinement, civility, formality and propriety inspire more refined responses and promote a general atmosphere of respect and consideration. The way that you appear to yourself influences your attitude and self-esteem, and the way you look to others suggests your appreciation for their sensitivities. Form and appearance are forces you can use to advantage without being empty, shallow or deceptive.

However, regardless of your appearance, the meaning or intent behind your actions reverberates throughout eternity. You cannot hide your intentions from cosmic law and on some level everyone is registering and responding to your motivations. Therefore, pay attention to your intentions and watch what you do; follow your sense of honor, integrity and respect.

Experience Represented by the Sphere

This Sphere represents your sense of *Honor* or integrity. It also represents the pure and sacred radiance which shines from every noble deed, igniting *the urge for perfection* which drives us to do better than our best, prompting us to grow, evolve and refine your self expressions. Sphere 8 is also associated with the intellectual-nature of the personality, including your abilities to think, communicate and rationalize. It also has to do with the forces of form and reverberation. In its highest sense, Sphere 8 represents the sacred nature of the Infinite which reverberates from the core of all creation, and which is *Hermetically sealed* in the lines of every form. Conditions and individuals represented by this Sphere are characterized by refinement, formality, intellectuality and respect. Experiences represented by this Sphere are teaching you to pay attention to matters of form, to use your intellectual faculties constructively and to honor and respect all beings.

Kabbalistic Correspondences

(use for your further insight and meditation)

The Divine Name associated with this Sphere is, *Elohim Tzabaoth*. This Name means, *Lord of Hosts*, and it represents the feminine polarity of the Divine Name of Sphere 7. *Elohim Tzabaoth* refers to the *Power of Sacredness*, or the *Power to Be Sacred* which inspires profound humility and submission to a higher purpose.

The Archangel associated with this Sphere is *Archangel Raphiel*. His name means, *Healing of God*. He represents the guiding will of your conscience which alerts you as to when you are dishonoring yourself or another, and which guides you back toward humility and self-respect along the path of reform.

The Angels associated with this Sphere are named *The Beni Elohim*. Their name means, *The Children of God*. They inspire you to be *like God*, or any higher ideal that you strive to emulate or live up to.

The Astrological Correspondence with this Sphere is the planet *Mercury*. Named after the Messenger of the Gods in ancient Greek mythology, Mercury is the astrological ruler of the intellect. The higher purpose of the intellect is to be an instrument through which the greater truths can be effectively hinted at and deduced.

The Type of Intelligence associated with this Sphere is called, *Perfecting*. This is because we must always strive to express our feelings and deepest urges in forms which convey them *perfectly*.

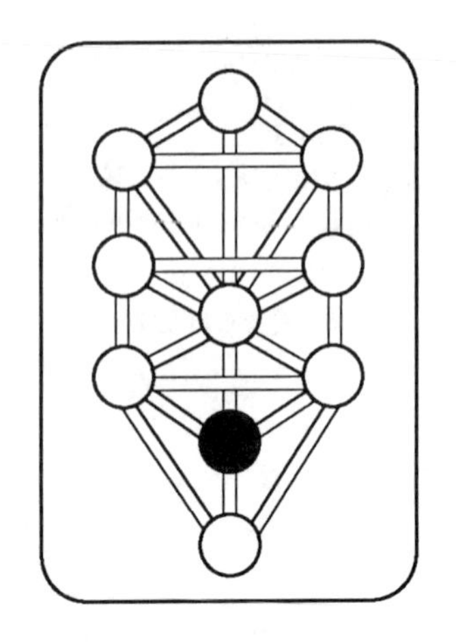

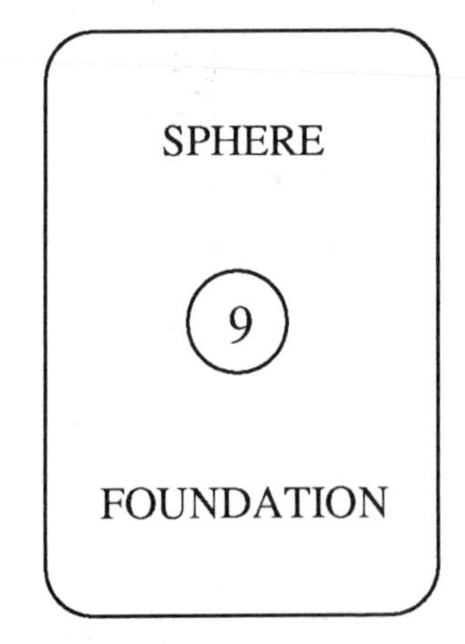

Hebrew Title: *Yesod* (pronounced: Yeh-sod)

Guidance of the Sphere

Examine established patterns to determine how well they are working for you in the present; replace those that now work against you. Rely upon trends from the past that are still working. The energy of momentum can open many doors that a new start would have to wait for.

Take your memories in hand. Release from those visions that stand in your way and impose a blockage to future progress. The past can only be repeated in your own mind.

Release from attachment to the journey's end and focus instead on the journey itself. What will be is a product of what is. What you do in the present determines the consequences you attract and the trends you set into motion.

Imagination sets into motion the patterns of physical manifestation. Imagining the way that you want things to be sets things moving in that direction. The way that you imagine a condition also determines your reaction to it. Imagination masquerades as truth until one is aware that one is imagining. Observe the activities of your imagination carefully and discover what you *imagine* to be true.

Everything that happens occurs on a foundation of preparation. If you are finding it difficult to progress as quickly as you would like, or if you are encountering delay, use the time to become better prepared for the outcome you are seeking.

Experience Represented by the Sphere

This Sphere represents the Foundation level of existence. A foundation is an underlying system or structure of support. There is a foundation level in all things. This Sphere is specifically associated with sexuality (the foundation of life), memory (the foundation of the present) and imagination (the foundation of reality as it will be), the contents of your unconscious (the foundation of your personality). In your unconscious is stored all of your past experiences as well as your responses to those experiences. This includes your deeply rooted fears, desires and beliefs. At the Foundation of your unconscious is the True Pattern of your development; this is the deepest motivation of your being. To the extent that you adhere to your True Pattern, whatever you do is bound to work out best. Conditions and individuals represented by this Sphere are characterized by stability, permanence, determination and familiarity. Experiences represented by this Sphere are teaching you to examine, purify and perfect the underlying support system on which your enterprise stands.

Kabbalistic Correspondences
(use for your further insight and meditation)

The Divine Name associated with this Sphere is, *Saddai el Chai*. This Name means, *Almighty Living God*. It represents the Power to live and procreate.

The Archangel associated with this Sphere is *Archangel Gabriel*. His name means, *Strength of God*. He is famous for the trumpet he blows which awakens the dead to new and higher life.

The Angels associated with this Sphere are named the *Ashim*. Their name means, *Souls of Fire*. They bring to you the thoughts and feelings which spring from your True Pattern and manifest the physical conditions that best reflect who you are.

The Astrological Correspondence with this Sphere is the *Moon*. There are so many reasons for this that a brief explanation seems inadequate to even attempt, while a more complete explanation would require too much space. Hopefully it will suffice to suggest that as the moon absorbs and projects the light of the Sun, so does your unconscious receive and project the guiding light of your True Self.

The Type of Intelligence associated with this Sphere is called, *Purifying* because whatever is not built on a firm foundation of truth or alignment with the cosmic will is not going to last.

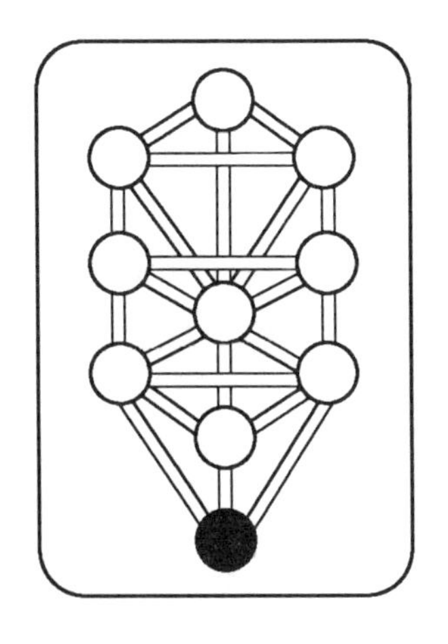

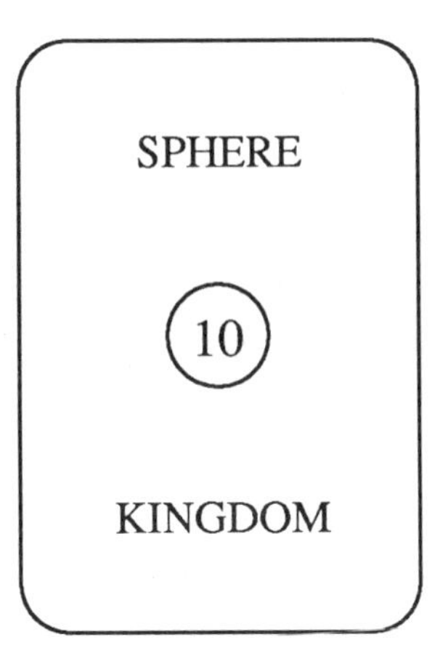

Hebrew Title: *Malkuth* (pronounced: Mahl-Kooth)

Guidance of the Sphere

When you can take matters no farther, bring things to a close. To attempt to force further advancement or improvement is simply to go around in circles until you reach stagnation. Trust in the product or outcome of your best efforts.

Examine physical appearances and conditions as a means of diagnosing their deeper meaning and hidden causes. The outer is a reflection of the inner; the present is a product of the past.

The physical stage is the last stage of creation. Until something has been brought to the physical level, the cycle of its purpose has not yet been completed. You must ground your visions into physical manifestations before you can move on to something new.

Bring your worthy ideas and intentions to the physical level. It generally requires more will to act or to produce than it does to think about what *may* work. However, until something is brought to the physical level it has not yet been fully tested, nor can it be expected to attract all of the rewards it deserves.

Some fear ending a project because they lack confidence in the repercussions. Letting your work go into the world, where its merit will be judged, is an act of faith. However, to resist this simply puts off the inevitable. You will never be certain of the outcome until you receive it; and even then, when the results are upon you, interpreting their meaning is entirely subjective.

How do you know that you are not already experiencing success? Perhaps all that is needed is for you to permit yourself to drop your striving for something more, and to recognize, enjoy and take more complete advantage of what you have available.

Experience Represented by the Sphere

The name of this Sphere is, *Kingdom.* It represents the physical or earthly plane of existence. Physical expression is the final stage of creation;. the physical plane is an outer expression of an inner process. Your activities on earth are a kind of proving-ground for your spiritual progress. Your outward, physical conditions are a sign or symbol pointing to the inner causes which brought them about. Conditions and individuals represented by this Sphere will tend to be characterized by materialism, rewards, success, completion, and an emphasis on the physical level. Experiences represented by this Sphere are teaching you how to diagnose causes from effects, as well as how to deal with endings and success.

Kabbalistic Correspondences

(use for your further insight and meditation)

The Divine Name associated with this Sphere is, *Adonai ha Aretz,* which means *God of the Earth.* The Divine Name, *Adonai Malak* is also associated with Sphere 10. This Name means, *God the King.* These Names refer to the Power to determine earthly manifestation or physical conditions.

The Archangel associated with this Sphere is *Archangel Sandalphon.* Taken literally, his name, which is Greek in origin, means, *One With Sandals,* suggesting his earthly quality. The Ancients taught that upon your sincere request *Sandalphon.* will bring to you whatever you need to help you on Earth.

The Angels associated with this Sphere are named *The Cherubim.* Their name means, *The Strong.* They uplift us by helping us to carry the earthly burdens that would otherwise oppress us.

The Astrological Correspondence with this Sphere is the *Earth* itself; more specifically, the four material elements of: earth, air, fire and water. These are the building-blocks of the physical plane. Kabbalists associate them with your four basic levels: spirituality (fire), mentality (air), emotionality (water) and physicality (earth). When these are balanced we attract good things.

The Type of Intelligence associated with this Sphere is called, *Resplendent* because physical conditions shed light on the inner cause, meaning or intention behind it.

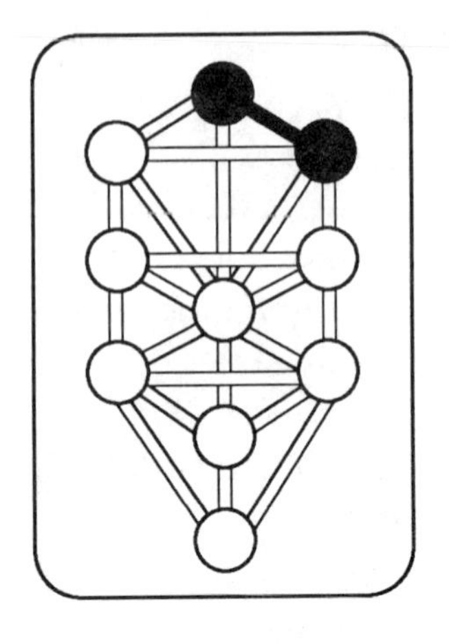

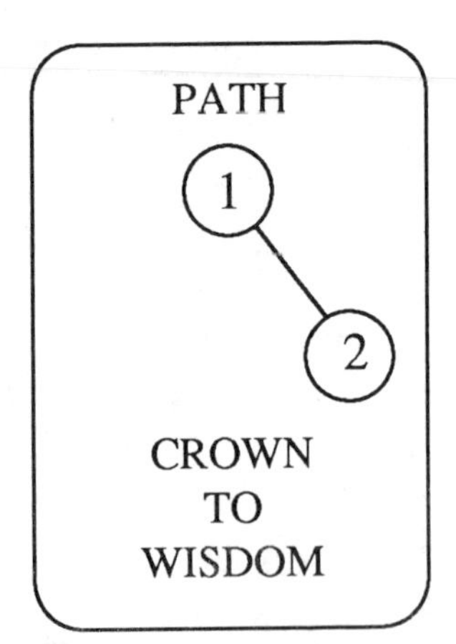

Guidance of the Path

The highest level of Wisdom is beyond consciousness. It rules the universe with Perfect Intelligence. To trust in It is to trust in yourself and in what you do. Whatever happens, have faith that it is exactly what you need and matters will work out even better than expected.

There *is* a Greater Power in the universe. It is in you and around you at all times. It is infinite, all-powerful and self-aware. There is no limit to what It can do, and It is the source or cause of all that is. When you acknowledge the existence of this Power and trust that It can work *for* you instead of *against* you, you awaken your subconscious connection with It.

The present is the threshold of the unknown. It is new, and any sense of familiarity with the past is merely superficial. You may comfort yourself at times with the presumption that your expectations are reliable, but they are not. You may hold yourself back from taking certain chances or accepting certain changes, when you really do not know what lies ahead.

You are confronting a new beginning. Your past should not be permitted to blindly determine your current choices. Fears of repeating the past are unfounded. Anything is possible at this point. One thing that you can count on is that things will turn out better than you expect, so expect the best.

Try the unpredictable; a new and different approach stimulaes growth and brings new life. Or, try old ones that did not work in the past; you may find they bring about a different result. Breaking routine is an act of humility. Accept that there is more than what you know. The unconventional or unusual may be an enemy to the status quo, but it is essential for continued progress and improvements.

Catch the essence of the spiritual fire which shines light on the infinite. Taking risks that contradict logic, public opinion, or even your basic, physical instincts becomes a kind of conduit through which the *ever mysterious* enters the world to stimulate change and awakening.

Here is the unknown. Do not bother trying to make sense of it. Rather, accept that you do not have the faintest notion of the truth. You have entered the land where the question, "Why?" has no meaning.

Experience Represented by the Path

This Path represents *your power to trust in a Greater Power.* This becomes necessary when you discover that you cannot know the facts you need to make an intelligent decision, when you realize that you must take a risk. On the spiritual journey, this Path represents the one constant: movement beyond the known. Individuals and conditions represented by this Path are characterized by the new and different, with an as yet undefined potential. Experiences represented by this Path are teaching you that you can only go so far based on what you know, and in order to go further you will have to take a leap of faith.

Kabbalistic Correspondences
(use for your further insight and meditation)

The Hebrew Letter associated with this Path is, *Aleph* (pronounced: Ah-leff). This is the first letter of the Hebrew Alphabet, suggesting new beginnings.
The Meaning of this letter is *Ox,* and *Life-Breath.* It suggests the endless strength and inspiration that empowers us to try again and start anew.
The Tarot Card associated with this Path is *Key 0, The Fool.* It pictures a youthful male about to step off a high cliff; but his face shows only fearless trust in a higher power. It suggests a leap of faith.
The Astrological Correspondence of this Path is the planet *Uranus,* having to do with originality, invention and revolutionary approaches.
The Type of Intelligence associated with this Path is called, *Fiery.* It corresponds with the spiritual fire in the core of our being which relentlessly drives us on to seek new challenges.

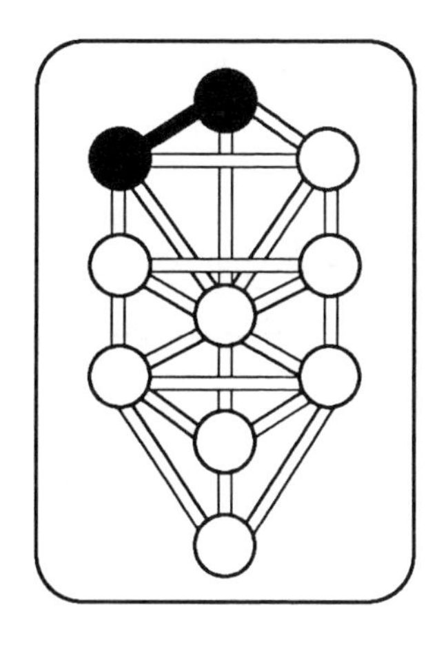

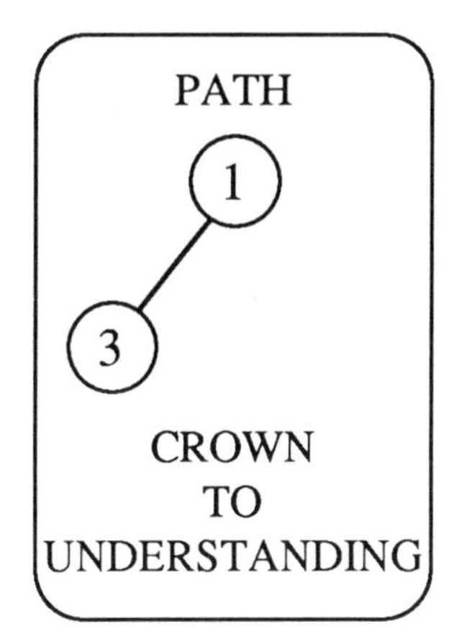

Guidance of the Path

By holding the mind steadily focused, directed upon a single point, the focal-point becomes transparent and inner meaning is revealed. This power of concentration is put to its greatest use when it is focused inward, toward the Higher Will of your True Self which is guiding you from the innermost core of your being.

Your energy will tend to follow the direction of your attention. Whatever you hold your attention on receives your power. It is therefor wise to be aware of what you are giving your attention to.

In most cases, until one has awakened sufficiently to the inner workings of the self, one's power of attention seemes to be ruled by external events which trigger automatic reactions of thought, desire and emotion. However, the rightful place of attention is as the master of these lower forces. If you hold attention on something you want, your desire for it is going to be stimulated. If you concentrate on a particular line of thought, you will soon notice a train of connecting ideas following one another along that line.

Place your attention under the direction of your will. Instead of acting and reacting blindly, decide on what you intend to achieve and concentrate on the process of its accomplishment. If your mind drifts in other directions, bring it back to a single-pointed focus on your objective. Gradually, your subconscious will receive your message and you will find things happening in line with your intention.

Experience Represented by the Path

This Path represents *your power of concentration,* or *attention ruled by will.* A wise one has said that when you become aware of what is running your attention you will discover what is running your life. What you intend, and what you give your attention to are important factors in your life because they significantly influence what happens to you. You need not be a victim of your intention and attention. Make them conscious and you gain control of them; you will naturally release them from lower attachments and make them available to serve higher, more intelligent purposes. As a result, the direction of your life will take on greater meaning. Individuals represented by this Path will tend to demonstrate initiative and intelligence. Conditions represented by this Path will tend to reveal deep mysteries and require a disciplined focus. Experiences represented by this Path are teaching you to take responsibility for your *intentions* and to take control of your *attention.*

Kabbalistic Correspondences
(use for your further insight and meditation)

The Hebrew Letter associated with this Path is *Beth.* It is the second letter of the Hebrew Alphabet and suggests *interior action.*

The Meaning of this letter is *House*, suggesting something you build to live in. What your entire life is, and two of the most powerful forces which build your life are your powers of intention and attention.

The Tarot Card associated with this Path is *Key 1, The Magician.* It pictures a dark-haired male standing with closed eyes in a garden. He is apparently looking within, focusing on his intentions. His right hand is holding a wand that is raised above his head. This symbolizes Higher Will. His left hand is pointing down to the garden floor, from where the plants and flowers which surround him grow. His act of down-pointing suggests that he is an instrument through which Higher Will does its work upon the earth. The garden is a symbol of the the earthly manifestations of that Higher Will.

The Astrological Correspondence of this Path is the planet Mercury. As stated earlier, this planet has to do with the intellect and is named after the Messenger of the Gods of ancient Greek mythology. It is associated with this Path partly because your intellect or brain is your *house* of mental light.

The Type of Intelligence associated with this Path is called *Transparent.* Concentration gradually reveals the *inner workings of whatever you focus upon.*

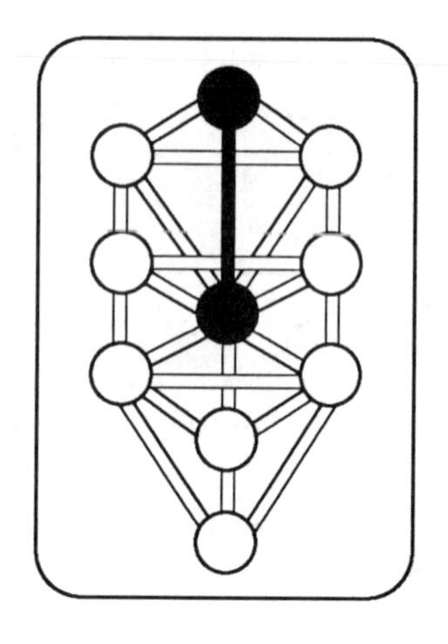

Guidance of the Path

Trust your own capacity to receive higher consciousness from within. If you need to know something, take the time to look within and remain open and receptive to what occurs to you. Sometimes, the best guidance that one can give to another is simply, "Use your own ability to receive from within yourself what you need to know".

Your subconscious mind is your connection with Higher Mind, which has unlimited potential. Be open to the knowledge you can receive within and, if it seems reasonable, test it out by applying it in your situation.

You only limit what you can know by the limits you believe in. The substance of your consciousness is like water in that it can take any shape. The more trusting, open and flexible you are to your mind's capacity to provide you with the solution to your problem, the more quickly that solution is likely to occur, and the more brilliant it is apt to be. State your problem or question clearly to yourself or simply focus your attention on what it is you need to know. Then, trust that your subconscious will reveal to you the knowledge it has which pertains to your need.

Remain emotionally balanced, calm and patient as you await the insight you require. The more relaxed you are, the more profoundly your subconscious responds to your direction. Stay alert; the subconscious responds to the conscious mind most subtly. If you are not vigilant, you may miss it.

Experience Represented by the Path

This Path represents *the power of your subconscious mind.* Your subconscious is your access to Higher Mind abilities. This includes personal and collective memories, higher understanding and more expansive awareness in general that is ordinarily beyond the range of your conscious mind. For instance, there is virtually nothing you can hide from anyone because their subconscious mind can detect it. Individuals and Conditions represented by this Path will tend to be characterized by unclarity and uncertainty which will require deep, intuitive sensing to figure out. Experiences represented by this Path are teaching you to patiently reflect upon matters to receive the knowledge, guidance or answers that you need.

Kabbalistic Correspondences
(use for your further insight and meditation)

The Hebrew Letter associated with this Path is *Gimel.* It is the third letter of the Hebrew alphabet. Kabbalists associate it with the production of ideas.

The Meaning of this letter is *Camel.* A camel was used by the ancient desert people to transport goods and information across long distances. This suggests the power of your subconscious to bring the knowledge to you that you need.

The Tarot Card associated with this Path is *Key 2, The High Priestess* It pictures a young woman seated between two pillars: one black, the other white. Behind her hangs a curtain, veiling what is behind it. Her open eyes seem extremely calm, yet alert. On her lap lies a partially unrolled scroll from which a stream like water flows down to the ground and out of the picture. The scene represents your power to access your subconscious ability to see or know what is hidden. The stream represents the endless supply of knowledge available through the subconscious when you know how to relate with it. Upon her head is poised an elaborate head-dress, with a white disc in the middle of two white crescents. The two crescents suggest the horns of a bull, the astrological symbol of Taurus, which represents the practicality of tapping the vast reaches of the subconscious, as well as the patience it requires.

The Astrological Correspondence of this Path is the Moon which is a symbol of the subconscious. As the moon receives the light of the sun to relieve the night of its darkness, so can the subconscious receive the light of Higher Mind to relieve us of the darkness of our ignorance.

The Type of Intelligence associated with this Path is called *Uniting* because your subconscious can extend your awareness beyond boundaries and unite you with all.

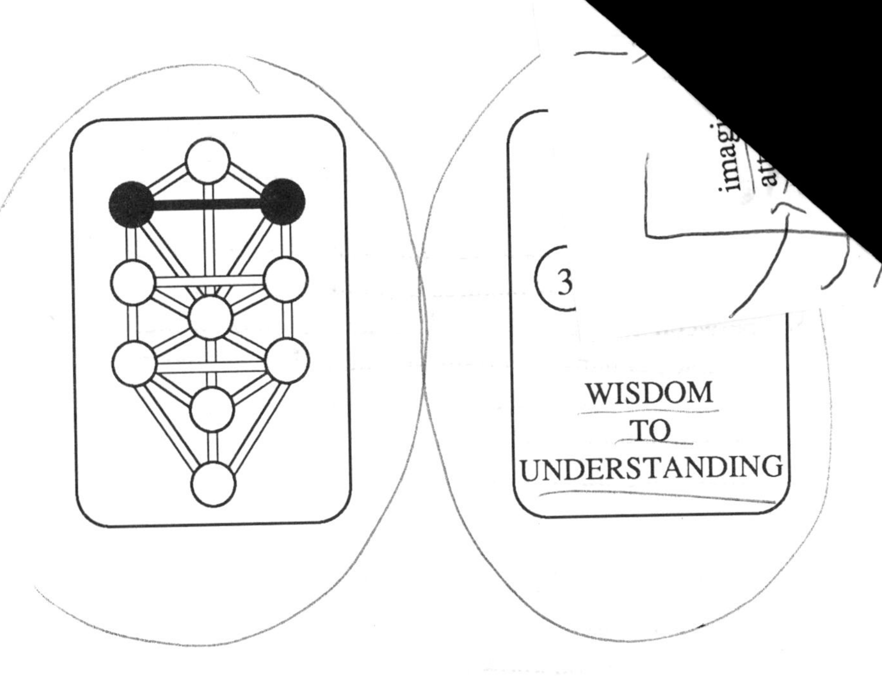

Guidance of the Path

Your desires and intentions plant seeds in your subconscious. These take root, grow and unfold as luminous ideas and visions in your creative imagination that guide you toward your goals and attract what you need to continue to progress.

Examine what is happening for any light it may shed on the feelings, imaginings, desires or intentions which may have attracted these circumstances to you. Allow your circumstances to show you what you *want* to happen. If things are not flowing in the direction that you want them to, or if the flow seems blocked, resist the urge to wax negative, or to enter into futile struggle that only raises your level of frustration. Instead, reconsider your desires and intentions. Be selective regarding those you focus your attention on and commit to. What you focus on gains strength.

The creative process begins with desire, intent and imagination. You cannot desire or intend what you do not [illegible]ne. Desire, intent and imagination are magnetic; they [illegible]tract a flow of external and internal circumstances that can help you to advance in the direction of their manifestation in physical reality. Changing your circumstances begins with adjusting the direction of your desires, intentions and creative imagination. Directing the flow of circumstances begins with directing the activity within.

Feelings, desires and intentions of a conflicting nature tend to attract blockages and opposition in physical manifestation. The fantasies you indulge in strengthen your feelings of attraction and repulsion. Heed the guidance of your higher will, wisdom and understanding in what you choose. Discipline yourself to drop the thoughts that incite your inner conflict and focus on accomplishing what you know is best. Take charge of the internal flows that attract the external circumstances of your life.

Experience Represented by the Path

This Path represents *the power of your Creative Imagination*. Imagining what you desire or intend attracts a flow of circumstances to you, both internal and external. Gaining authority over your creative imagination gives you more authority over the direction of your life. Individuals often resist the intelligence of taking charge of their inner life because they regard their problems and objectives as external. They therefore look for external ways to change things, but this constitutes a focus on symptoms rather than causes, because the outer is a reflection of the inner. Conditions and individuals represented by this Path will tend to stimulate the imagination and arouse desires; they are also likely to be a reflection of secret feelings which you need to become more aware of. Experiences represented by this Path are teaching you to become conscious of your creative imagina-

tion and of your inner life in gener
influence that the inner has on the

Kabbalistic Corresp

(use for your further insight and meditation)

The Hebrew Letter associated with this Path is *Daleth* (pronounced: Dah-leth). It is associated with the forces of fertility.

The Meaning of this letter is *Door*. As a door permits entry and exit from a house, the creative images which flow *out* from your consciousness draw *back to you* the circumstances they attract.

The Tarot Card associated with this Path is *Key 3, The Empress*. It pictures an attractive young woman seated on a stone bench. She is subtly pregnant and holds a staff of authority in front of her womb. Twelve stars hover around her head and she is surrounded by a field of wheat, grass and trees. Emerging from behind her to her left is a bunch of red roses. Behind her a stream flows into the picture, across her back, and cascades at her left into a pool at her feet. This image represents life, creativity, attraction and fruitfulness.

The Astrological Correspondence of this Path is Venus. Named after the Greek goddess of love, Kabbalists associate this planet with the energies of fecundity, attraction, imagination and desire.

The Type of Intelligence associated with this Path is called *Luminous*. Our inner states radiate out and draw to us the events we receive.

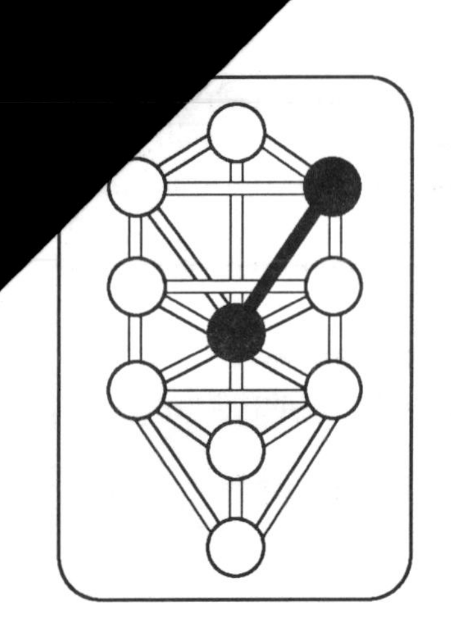

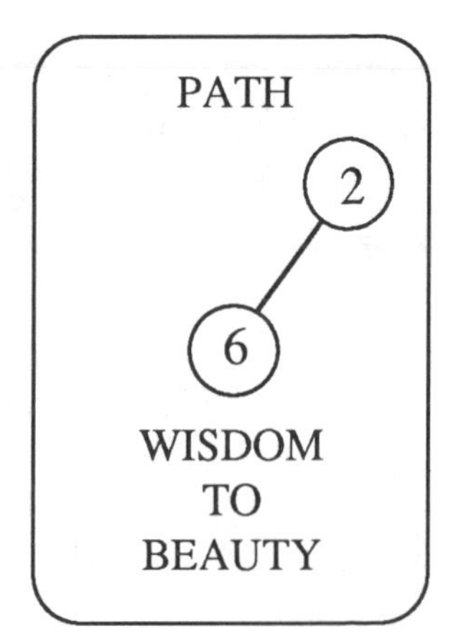

Guidance of the Path

Take matters in hand. Oversee what is happening until you get a clear idea of what is going on. Then, focus on your objective and take action that is strategically determined to advance you toward your goal.

Balance love with reason to guide your activities. Think about what you intend to accomplish before taking steps to achieve it. Then, take action consistent with your aim or purpose.

Be patient, not insistent on achieving everything in a single stroke. While you can direct the flow of circumstances by taking action, you will have to be satisfied with whatever degree of progress you can make. Following each effort, reassess your position. From there, take the next step.

Assume the attitude of *authority* over your actions and your situation. Continue to apply directed action until you have taken things as far as they can go. You will not be deflected by the forces that oppose your progress if you hold the focus of your intent and continue moving toward it. Do not be dismayed by opposition. Respond with intelligently directed action. Avoid reacting emotionally, automatically, wildly. Find your opening and move through it. If you do not see an opening, take action aimed at creating it.

Whatever you intend to accomplish, it will require you to use your skills. Skill shapes action in line with what you intend that action to accomplish.

Experience of the Path

This Path represents *your power to direct activity with intelligence and skill.* This may seem like an all too obvious power to consider as profound; and yet, it is a life-wisdom key which is rarely understood in a way that reveals its profound significance. You do not *need* to *re*-act the way that you do. Your actions determine what happens to you. A wise one has defined life as, "The reactions to your actions". If you think before you act, and act as skillfully as possible in line with a plan for accomplishment, your actions will tend to be more effective in bringing about what you intend. Individuals and conditions represented by this Path are characterized by perceptiveness, organization, skills and supervision. The experiences represented by this Path are teaching you to develop and apply skills, initiative, strategy and self-control.

Kabbalistic Correspondences

(use for your further insight and meditation)

The Hebrew Letter associated with this Path is *Heh.* It is associated with speech, which is the most obvious example of intelligence expressed in physical action.

The Meaning of this letter is *Window*. A window is a means of observation. Observing the field of activity before applying action is the basis for intelligent action.

The Tarot Card associated with this Path is *Key 4, The Emperor*. It pictures a bearded male dressed in military garb; he wears a helmet and other pieces of armor in strategic places for protection, including a metal breastplate, knee-guards and metal foot-guards. He is seated on a cube with a ram pictured on one of its sides, symbol of the Astrological sign of Aries. He holds a staff of authority in his right hand; in his left he holds a globe. His head is turned to his right, so that only his left eye is showing as he gazes steadily in that direction. His seat is on a raised portion of earth, and he seems to be overlooking a stream that flows into and out of the picture behind and below him. On the opposite side of the stream stands a mighty mountain of crystal clear ice. This scene symbolizes the power to intelligently direct, regulate and supervise activity.

The Astrological Correspondence of this Path is the constellation *Aries,* which is Latin for *ram*. Astrologers associate Aries with the impulse to act and it is said to rule the head on the physical body. One who *heads* something is in charge of its activities.

The Type of Intelligence associated with this Path is called, *Constituting,* because it represents the power to see things clearly before responding to them.

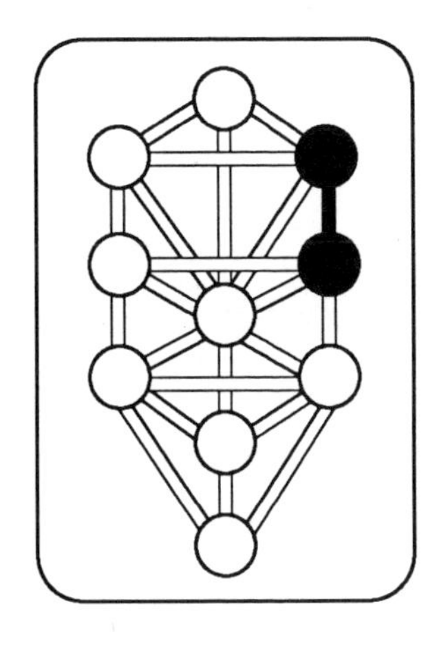

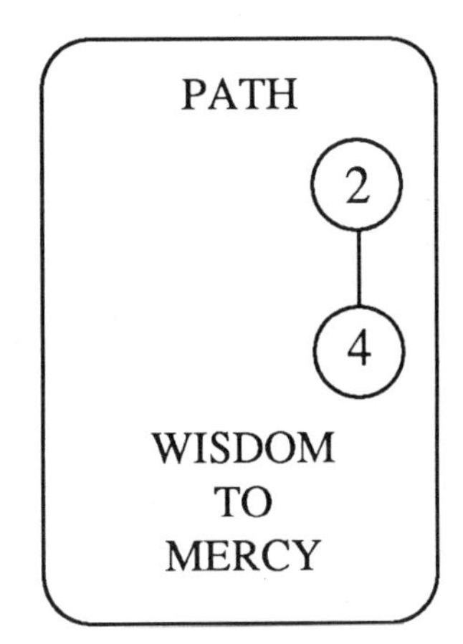

Guidance of the Path

Take hold of your inner light. Base your choices on your inner guidance and build your life upon it. If you do what you know in your heart is right, you will not have to go through the losses which will teach you to follow what you knew. Trust the inner guidance which points the way to genuine stability, security and peace.

Within you is a spiritual guide or teacher. It is ready to help you when you reach a spiritual cross-road. You cannot go in two directions at once. Your inner teacher has but one counsel: choose the path of spiritual gain at the cost of worldly interests when it becomes clear that you must give-up one for the sake of the other. This does not mean that your genuine inner guidance will ever be impractical. As long as you live on earth your spiritual growth has worldly needs. It will always guide you toward the worldly conditions that are most conducive to your real advancement in life, helping you to build a safe and secure worldly foundation on which to base your spiritual life with a minimum of worldly distraction.

Willingness, humility, surrender, and submission are the keys to making choices that will bring about real progress and lasting gain. If you do not know the correct course to take it is probably because you are resisting knowing. We fear to know what is best when we believe that it may force us to lose or to give-up something or someone we have grown attached to. The wise have always taught us to free ourselves of our worldly attachments for this very reason. If you are confronting an attachment that is causing you to be confused, begin working on releasing that attachment now. This is not an external process of physically letting-go, but an internal one of building trust in the place of fear. It is useless to try to hear what you are unwilling to listen to.

Experience Represented by the Path

This Path represents your power to make choices that increase your *spiritual* resources. You can receive the most practical, inner guidance in any situation by asking yourself this simple question: "What is the best way for me to deal with this situation for my spiritual growth?" Having asked that question, remain open and receptive to your inner voice, the guiding light of your growing, spiritual nature. We are deafened to this "voice of silence" by our worldly attachments, which make us unwilling or resistant to its guidance out of fear. Individuals and conditions represented by this Path are characterized by a deep, underlying connection to something higher. Experiences represented by this Path are teaching you to base your choices on what is best for your spiritual growth, and to consider the issue of practicality from a deeper, more spiritual perspective.

Kabbalistic Correspondences

(use for your further insight and meditation)

The Hebrew Letter associated with this Path is *Vau* (pronounced: Vuv). It is associated with thought.

The Meaning of this letter is *Nail.* A nail is used by builders to securely fasten things together, just as your spiritual, inner guidance guides you in building your life on secure ground.

The Tarot Card associated with this Path is *Key 5 , The Hierophant.* A hierophant is a spiritual teacher. This image pictures a male seated on a throne in a pontiff's regalia. His throne is on a dais, before which two monks stand side-by-side, with their backs to us and facing their guide. Their gestures portray submission, surrender and reverence toward his wise and sacred counsel. On the teacher's throne are the horns of a bull, the symbol of the astrological sign of Taurus. Taurus is associated with practicality, suggesting to us that the guidance of the spiritual teacher within is practical in the very deepest sense.

The Astrological Correspondence of this Path is the constellation *Taurus,* for the sense of patience and practicality that is associated with it.

The Type of Intelligence associated with this Path is called, *Triumphant and Eternal* because those who make choices that are guided by their sense of spiritual growth find those choices working out best and leading to the most lasting and significant gains.

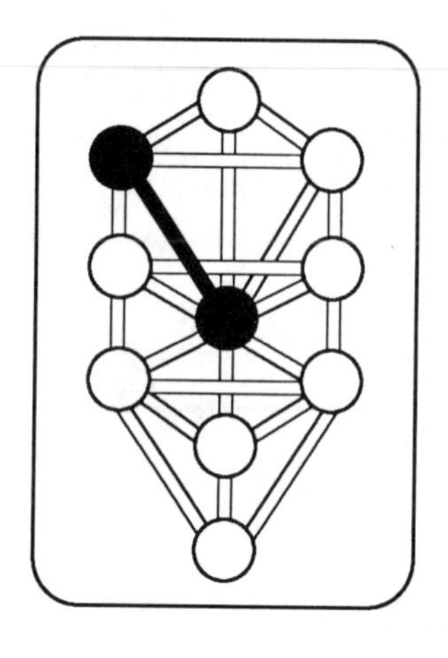

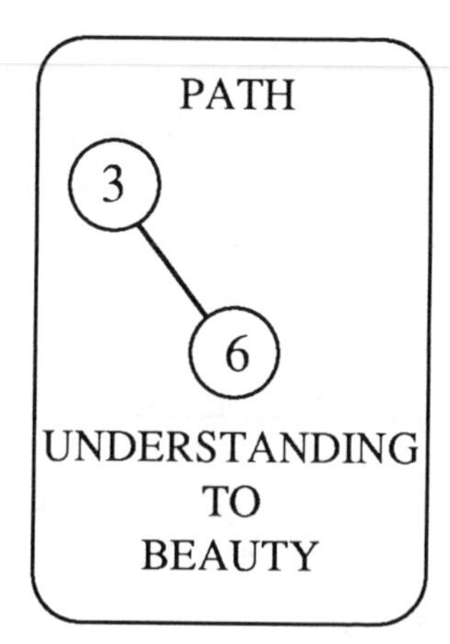

Guidance of the Path

Pay attention to externals, but do not look to them alone in your choices and decisions. Your powers of reason and observation can only take you so far. This is why the ancients regarded reason and the physical senses as shrouds of darkness rather than as portals of light. Danger lurks behind the fruits of worldly desire, in the fires of worldly ambition, in the false illumination of the materialistic arguments of the rational mind. To move beyond your current set of limitations, trust in something deeper.

The personal ego is being tempted by its hunger for control and understanding. While these are noble in themselves, the real motivation is to give yourself a false sense power and superiority.

To find your True Inner Directive, remain open to receiving the guiding light of something deeper, and distance yourself from those lower forces which masquerade as realistic guiding light.

Be discriminating toward the internal forces you align yourself with. If you submit to superficial drives and tendencies, you disconnect yourself from the higher consciousness which alone can guide you according to your *Real Disposition.* Go deeper within in search of the Real You. Balance and unite the masculine and the feminine in you to give birth to the sense of who *you* really are. Use your masculine strength to take action and your feminine strength to be receptive to a higher level of guidance than you can entirely explain or immediately make sense of.

Experience Represented by the Path

This Path represents *your power of discrimination.* You are not bound to react to every impulse that arises in you, nor to blindly follow the dictates of superficial reason. Use your power of discrimination to help you to recognize and to follow the more reliable guidance of the deeper, impelling urge of the *Real You.* Individuals and conditions represented by this Path will tend to involve certain complications due to conflicting trends and contradictory patterns. The experience represented by this Path is teaching you to examine yourself carefully in order to base your choices on something deeper than superficial reasoning or a sudden impulse of desire.

Kabbalistic Correspondences
(use for your further insight and meditation)

The Hebrew Letter associated with this Path is *Zain.* This letter is associated with the principle of movement.

The Meaning of this letter is *Sword.* A sword suggests separation, sharp definition, penetration. All are implicit in the concept of discrimination.

The Tarot Card associated with this Path is *Key 6 , The Lovers*. It pictures a nude male and female standing apart. Between them and in the distance a high mountain rises. Between them and above is a guardian angel; it is Archangel Michael (see: **Sphere 6** under, **Archangel**). Above and behind the archangel is a tremendous image of the Spiritual Sun. The male looks out across the level plane before him, while the female looks up in surrender and submission to Michael's guiding light. Behind the male is a tree with flames upon its branches, symbolizing the flames of ambition that will burn him if follows it. Behind the female is a tree with five ripe fruits representing the five senses and the objects of their desire; but a serpent waits in hiding there, ready to strike. The image is reminding you to base your choices on the deeper guiding impulse of your *True Self* in making choices.

The Astrological Correspondence of this Path is the constellation *Gemini,* which is Latin for, *Twins.* Gemini is associated with the forces of the intellect, especially with regard to what is referred to as the concrete mind, which the lovers in the Tarot image are being guided to rise above.

The Type of Intelligence associated with this Path is called, *Disposing*. This is because all choices that are based on one's *True* or *Higher Disposition*, as distinguished from the more superficial patterns of thought, desire and action, have the best chance of working out.

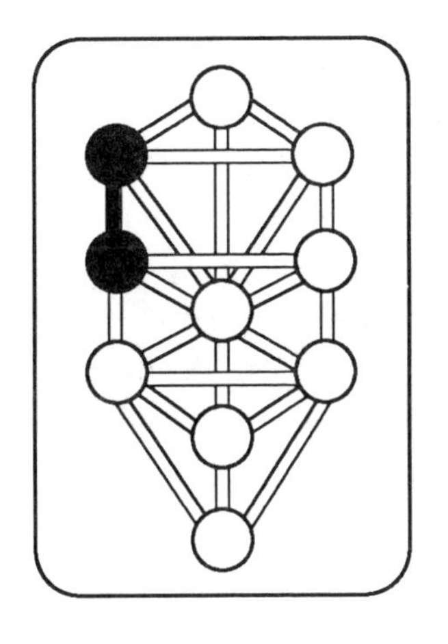

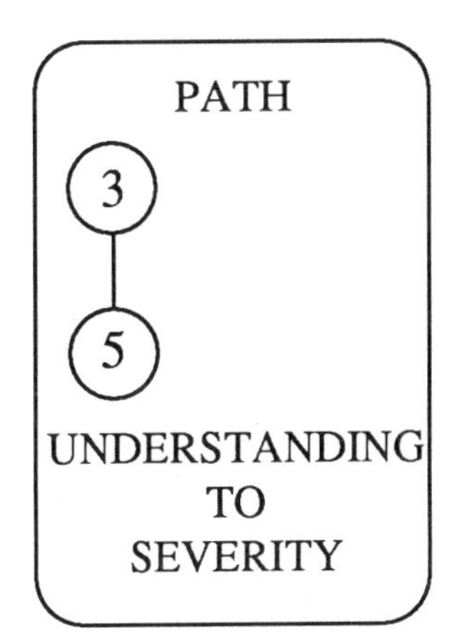

Guidance of the Path

The ability to *stop*, to stand and hold your ground physically, emotionally and mentally is a great skill worth the effort to win. There is no point in moving when there is no direction worth taking. Keep your thoughts, feelings, speech and actions in neutral until you can apply them in an intelligent direction.

The motion and commotion of scattered, superficial thoughts, speech, emotions and activity are influences of interference that limit clear understanding and block sound judgement. Moods affect your receptivity. If you are feeling high or low you are more susceptible to the destructive influences of your environment as well as those which stem from your own past habits. Therefore, concentrate on your inner peace and stillness *before* bringing your influence to bear on your circumstances.

Take into account the fact that the thoughts, feelings and attitudes of those around you are impinging upon you.

Every individual radiates how they are. Before responding to an urge, impulse or idea first check to make certain that it is *yours*, that it works for *you* and that its truth arises out of the depths of your own being. This builds a kind of fence of protection around you. Remember that you are an individual and you must protect your individuality to be true to yourself. You have your own star of destiny and your own ways of doing things. Have the courage to be original and lose the false need to fit in, to be accepted or even to be understood.

Alertness is your armor, and will is the reins by which you can steer the chariot of your own destiny. Choose non-reactivity until you see an intelligent way to respond. Realize that you are responsible for the consequences of whatever you say, think, feel or do. Another may insist, plead or even command - but your choice of response is *your* responsibility.

Experience Represented by the Path

This Path represents *your power to detach from inferior influences* in order to ready yourself to receive and to follow a more intelligent vision. It also refers to your power to be true to yourself despite the pressures others may put on you to be more agreeable or to live up to their expectations. Conditions and individuals represented by this Path will tend to warrant careful scrutiny and self-restraint. Experiences represented by this Path are teaching you that being true to yourself requires the strength to resist doing what others want or expect, as well as the strength to resist your own unbalanced moods and impulses.

Kabbalistic Correspondences

(use for your further insight and meditation)

The Hebrew Letter associated with this Path is *Cheth*. This letter is associated with sight.

The Meaning of this letter is *Fence*. The purpose of a fence is to keep certain influences in and others out.

The Tarot Card associated with this Path is *Key 7, The Chariot*. It pictures a vigilant male in warrior attire. He stands in a chariot that is motionless. In front of the chariot are two sphinxes, one black and the other white. They are not harnessed to the chariot but appear to be the sources of its locomotion. The charioteer holds a staff of authority in his right hand, while his left seems to be holding a set of reins, but there are no reins visible. Behind him there is a stream, behind that a high wall and behind that a city. The suggestion is one of individuality, as well as separation, disconnection or detachment from the external influences which would determine his direction of movement.

The Astrological Correspondence of this Path is the constellation *Cancer*, which is Latin for *crab*. Cancer is associated with physical and emotional sensitivity, as well as the tendency to insulate oneself from disturbing influences.

The Type of Intelligence associated with this Path is called, *Intelligence of the house of influence* because it represents your power to recognize and remain free from influences that would steer you off a more intelligent course.

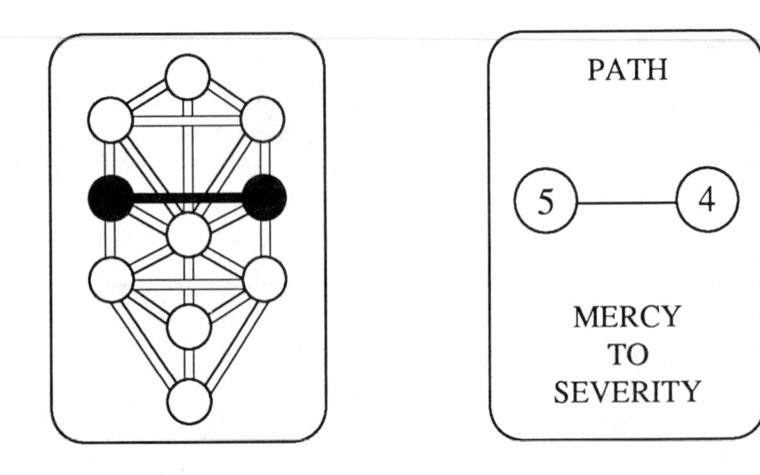

Guidance of the Path

How do you respond to your impulse to react? You have a choice, you know. You do not have to react in the way that your initial impulse determines. Observe your impulse to say something, to think about something, to indulge in a feeling or to take physical action of some kind. *Before* responding to that impulse reconsider your aim or purpose. Regardless of how strong that impulse is, you do not have to be controlled by it. Your drives and desires need not usurp the power to direct your life which rightfully belongs to your higher will.

When the impulse to react is strong it seems that the power to do anything else is weak by comparison. For example, if someone says something we do not like, the urge is to "rip his head off". The more tolerant, constructive approach is far more gentle. You might speak softly as you attempt to complete what you have started together, overlooking the other's crude remark. Apply gentle, persistent pressure in the direction that you intend things to go. Rise above the forces and conditions that arise to block your way. Concentrate on constructing something better rather than battling against something worse.

It is an act of utmost humility to be non-resistant toward uncooperative, unsupportive trends and individuals. Those who take antagonism personally feel the need to become angry, upset and frightened when things do not happen as they wish. You can rise above that petty need to be treated differently. Humble, forward movement can take you to the highest levels of attainment.

Your influence can succeed in transforming any adversity into advantage if it is applied with love, intelligence and patience. In the process, you yourself will be transformed; your higher, more loving and intelligent impulses and tendencies will grow stronger.

Experience Represented by the Path

This Path represents *your power to rise above your lower nature and strengthen your Higher Nature which can do all things in love, will and wisdom.* This occurs as you draw the energy out of the control of your more crude, destructive impulses and direct that energy into more intelligent, loving, patient action. This process is called,*Transmutation.* To transmute means to take something of lesser worth and transform it into something of greater worth. Individuals and conditions represented by this Path will tend to be characterized by a release of great power and an opportunity for mild change, progress or improvement. The experience represented by this Path is teaching you how to apply gentle measures of control aimed at creating something better.

Kabbalistic Correspondences

(use for your further insight and meditation)

The Hebrew Letter associated with this Path is *Teth.* This letter is associated with hearing.

The Meaning of this letter is *Serpent.* A serpent is a symbol of humble, subtle action that carries great power, as when it winds on its belly through the grass to surprise its victim with a mighty shock. (The serpent also symbolizes spiritual growth, as when our forces spiral upward to give birth and unfoldment to our higher powers, resulting in spiritual enlightenment.)

The Tarot Card associated with this Path is *Key 8, Strength.* It pictures a gentle woman stooping over a mighty lion. She seems fearless as she gently holds the lion's jaws open wide, exposing its long tongue and great teeth. Its huge claws look dangerous. Its tail rises in the air like a serpent. Around its neck a vine of roses winds and travels up the woman's spine until it reaches the top of her head winding around it like a crown. Above her head a figure-eight lies on its side, symbol of infinity. In the background a high mountain reaches into the sky, symbol of attainment. This scene portrays the transmutation process.

The Astrological Correspondence of this Path is the constellation *Leo,* Latin for *lion.* Astrologers associate Leo with powers of leadership. The greatest leaders are those who, led by their higher natures, lead others to their own higher potentials.

The Type of Intelligence associated with this Path is *Intelligence of the secret of all spiritual activities.* This *secret* is the *transmutation process* which in essence is real spiritual growth and development.

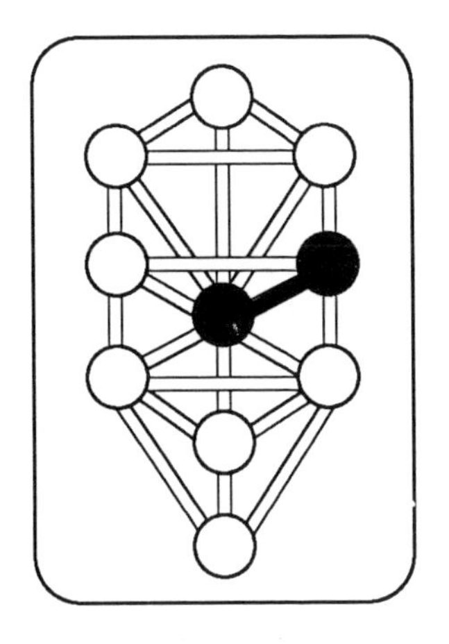

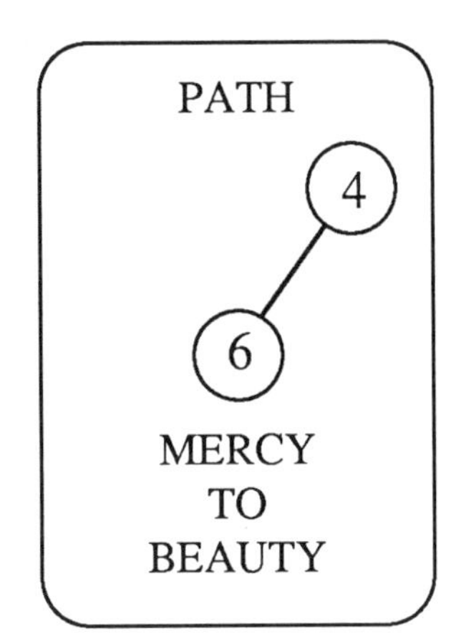

Guidance of the Path

Be as a light that shines with your own highest influences. Use your will to insist upon *your own* best efforts. There is no need to oppose anyone, nor to directly oppose the trend of events. Be as detached and disinterested in what is going on as is necessary for you to focus mainly on raising the quality of your response to the highest possible level.

Who are you, really? Identify yourself with your higher potential. Then, be less concerned with how others are acting, and more concerned with being true to yourself.

There is a point where we must be unconcerned with how we are received by others, or with the impact our actions have upon them. This is not to suggest that we are to be less compassionate. It is more a matter of respecting their free will as you concentrate on living up to your own standards. Another way of stating this is to strive to express beauty as you see it rather than playing to the audience driven by the false need for their approval.

Reserve judgement of yourself and others, and resist the urge to criticize or condemn. Keep a close watch on yourself for the purpose of higher self expression, not lower self-regard. Keep your inner eye focused on the ideal you are striving to achieve and it will naturally draw you toward it.

Protect yourself with wisdom; there is no weapon superior to it. Your own ability to make intelligent choices will take you where you want to go. To the summits of achievement go the wise. It is wise to place your best foot forward.

Experience Represented by the Path

This Path represents *your power to identify with your Higher Self.* The keys to accomplishing this are your will and self-awareness. Use your will to drop the habit of trying to change, control and manipulate *others.* As the sages teach: "You give away your power to reach your own higher potential by insisting on others changing to make you happy". Observe your own actions and reactions, and use your will to function at your highest potential. This is a never ending process of taking oneself higher and higher into the purified realms at the summits of wisdom. Individuals and conditions representd by this Path will tend to require a special effort to express one's best, but with that exists a special opportunity to do so. Experiences represented by this Path are teaching you to focus on raising *yourself,* improving the way *you* do things, instead of criticizing and condemning others or your circumstances.

Kabbalistic Correspondences

(use for your further insight and meditation)

The Hebrew Letter associated with this Path is *Yod.* It is associated with work.

The Meaning of this letter is *Hand.* A hand is a symbol of that which shapes a malleable substance, and this Path represents your Power to change the shape of yourself with your will.

The Tarot Card associated with this Path is *Key 9, The Hermit.* It pictures a solitary, bearded male figure standing on a mountain peak. The perimeter of the snow-covered summit bounds him closely. In his right hand he holds a lamp aglow with a six-pointed star, symbol of the Light of the Spiritual Sun. His left hand grips a staff, symbolizing will. Its highest point is just taller than he is, symbolizing his higher potential. It stands vertically before him, his forehead pressed upon it. He wears a heavy, gray cloak (symbolizing wisdom) to protect him from the harshness of the heights. His eyes are closed in a gesture of solemn intent. This image symbolizes your Power to achieve identification with your Higher Self.

The Astrological Correspondence of this Path is the constellation *Virgo,* which is Latin for, *virgin.* Astrologers associate Virgo with the urge to achieve purity and to express perfection.

The Type of Intelligence associated with this Path is called, *Intelligence of Will,* because it strives to align with the Will behind Creation.

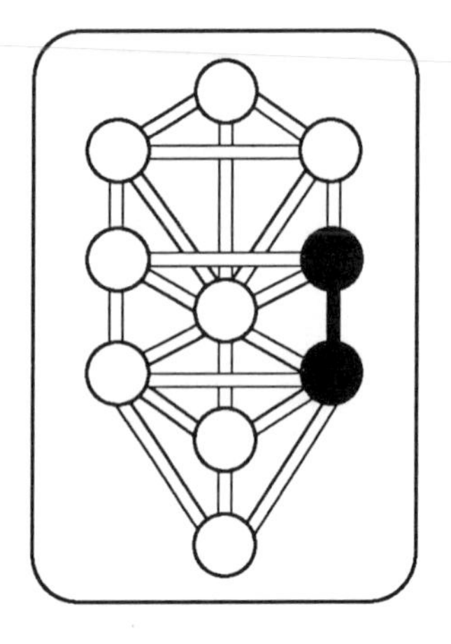

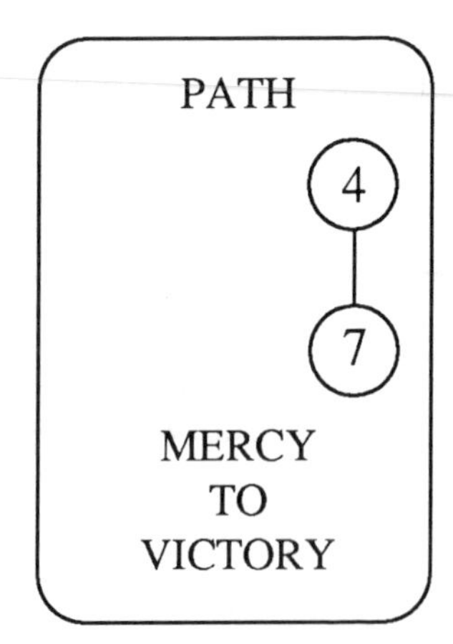

Guidance of the Path

Know what you intend to accomplish, use your will and dare to go for it. Waste none of your motivation talking about it until the job is done. Silence was the ancients' sacred key for directing the wheel of destiny. However, there are bound to be alternating cycles of opportunity and opposition. To expect a smooth ride without bumps or hitches is unbalanced and unrealistic optimism.

While you can expect things to go up and down, setbacks need not deter you from your chosen course. When things are getting out of hand relax your hold and drop your expectations. Avoid depending upon anything happening in any particular way. Trust that whatever is too difficult to change or to control is adequate the way that it is.

Remain alert to seize opportunities for advancement, to side-step avoidable pitfalls and to withdraw yourself from paths that lead astray. To some degree the forces of "luck" or fate are in charge of the outcome or final product of your efforts. This is because there is no way to have absolute control, and there is no telling how high or how low you will be in the cycle when it is time to move on to something new.

In a sense, there is a contradiction or paradox at work here. You are advised to apply the formula for directing your destiny, but at the same time to sit loose to life, to roll with the punches and to trust in the adequacy of what actually happens. These two approaches do not negate eachother. Combined they equal balance, the balance of flexible trust with assertive self-determination. Do your best and expect to win. However, avoid being carried away positively or negatively whcn things seem to be going with you or against you. Ultimately, this balanced approach will bring you an adequate approximation of exactly what you seek.

Experience Represented by the Path

This Path represents *your power to master the cosmic laws of cycle and return.* There is no such thing as a missed opportunity. Everything is cyclic; everything returns. You will have another chance. It is therefor unwise to clutch too tightly to that which is passing, or to reach too forcefully for what you cannot have for now. What you strive for you will receive, if not this time, perhaps next time; if not then, the time after. Gain and loss spin like a wheel. With each new turn we learn new lessons and gain new strength, until at last we have grown to be able to receive what we could not have handled sooner. Conditions and individuals represented by this Path can be characterized as risky, but with high potential. The experience represented by this Path is teaching you to accept what happens as exactly what you need, and to avoid taking anything too seriously.

Kabbalistic Correspondences

(use for your further insight and meditation)

The Hebrew Letter associated with this Path is *Kaph.* It is said to preside over life.

The Meaning of this letter is *Palm* or *Grasping Hand.* To hold onto something you must close your hand, which rejects the entry of something bigger and better. Trust life to make available to you that which is best for you to have.

The Tarot Card associated with this Path is *Key 10, The Wheel of Fortune.* It pictures a wheel in the sky symbolizing the cyclic motions of life. Around the wheel, at each of the four corners of the image, occurs a head. In the upper left is the head of a man, symbolizing the power to know. In the upper right is an eagle's head, symbol of the power to will. In the lower right is a lion's head, symbol of the power to dare. In the lower left is the head of a bull, symbol of the power to do in silence and patience until the job is done. Above the wheel is a sphinx with a sword, symbolizing secret knowledge and detachment. Going down one side of the wheel is a serpent, and going up the other is the Jackal-headed God, Anubis; these symbolize the alternation of positive and negative fortune, and the Sphinx represents the wisdom to stay above them both.

The Astrological Correspondence of this Path is the planet Jupiter. Astrologers associate Jupiter with expansion, luck and opportunity, as well as a generous, forgiving attitude.

The Type of Intelligence associated with this Path is called, *Rewarding*. It represents your power to direct as well as accept the turn of your wheel of fortune.

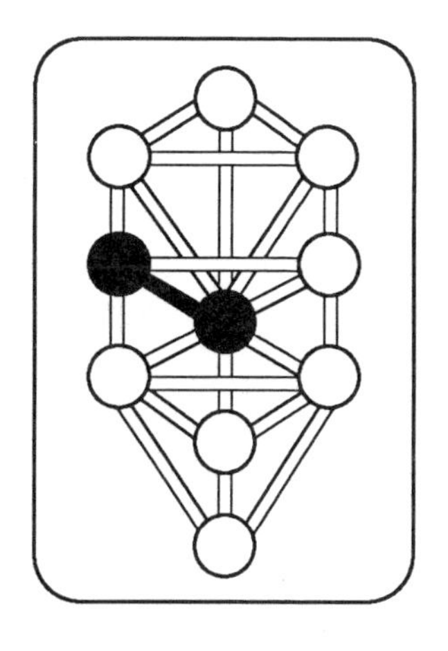

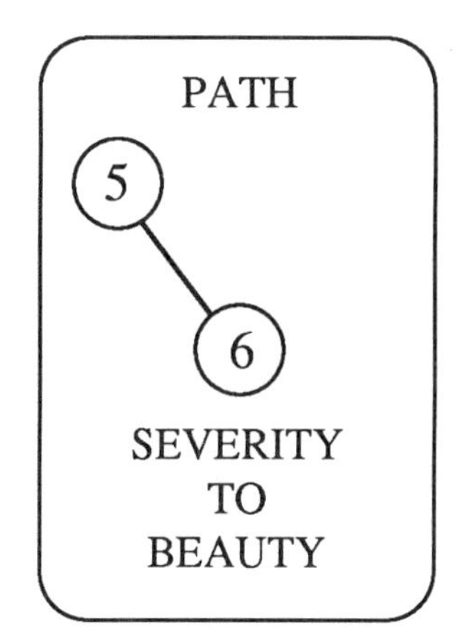

Guidance of the Path

Continue moving forward through your losses. This builds a momentum that develops inner strength.

There is no way to advance into the new without the old being taken away. If you are looking for a choice that will not involve a price that must be paid, your search is in vain.

Faith is a balancing force. Rely upon faith to help you to keep emotionally balanced during times of trial. Have faith that things can and will work-out in the end.

Be less concerned with how fairly or unfairly others are treating you, and more concerned with the quality of your own judgement. The way out of injustice is through justice. Consider matters carefully and be willing to accept or impose necessary hardship, difficulty or unpleasantness if that is what is required for a worthwhile purpose.

When one cannot know the consequences of one's actions all one has to go on is the quality of the act itself. Although there may be no visible evidence to support it, place your faith in your best efforts. Your future depends upon *your* choices and no one else's.

Think of the pressures of hardship as the earth's pressure on a piece of coal. It is producing a far stronger, more beautiful, enlightened individual. This may not be apparent during the early stages of difficulty, but in time one does discover the Greater Love that is at work.

Be excited in confrontations with your shortcomings and weaknesses. They foreshadow your greater growth. What you cannot do or endure with peace today will be relatively easy for you tomorrow. Your growth is the purpose of life, and your pain is telling you, "It is time to move on."

Listen to your heart as well as to your mind. Bring the two together in balance and you will find the path to peace.

Experience Represented by the Path

This Path represents *your power to overcome every kind of loss, hardship or adversity which life can possibly give to you.* When losses cut deep enough they take our faith. When you are suffering the most you will find that the pain only becomes unbearable when you have lost faith that things can work-out. However, eventually things begin to ease-up and improve and ultimately we realize that a purpose was served and we are healed, the wounds turned to compassion, and the pain turned into deeper wisdom and better judgement. Your power to make it through the deepest valleys and darkest nights is *faith,* which gives you the strength to make wise and loving choices. Individuals and conditions represented by this Path will tend to be characterized by little room for error, and by swift, unyielding reactions to one's actions. The experiences represented by this Path can be the most difficult one must pass through; they force us to rely on our faith.

Kabbalistic Correspondences

(use for your further insight and meditation)

The Hebrew Letter associated with this Path is *Lamed* (pronounced: Lah-med). It is said to preside over *The hall of birth.*

The Meaning of this letter is *Ox Goad.* The ox goad is a stick used to prod the ox to move forward, symbolizing the deeper purpose of our pain and losses in life, which prod us on toward growth and to make improvements.

The Tarot Card associated with this Path is *Key 11, Justice.* It pictures a figure seated between two pillars. The figure could be male or female, so balanced are the energies expressed by the physical features. The individual holds a sword in the right hand and a set of perfectly balanced scales in the left. In the Background is a set of heavy curtains with a space in the middle through which light can be seen. The individual's seat is raised up on a platform, suggesting that we are judged by the laws of a higher level, preparing us to enter it. As a whole the image represents the perfect power of balance and justice which is often concealed, but which is always at work, guiding us to growth and improvement.

The Astrological Correspondence of this Path is the constellation, Libra. Astrologers associate Libra with the forces of balance, justice and decision-making.

The Type of Intelligence associated with this Path is called, *Faithful,* because maintaining faith through hardship brings about the greatest spiritual advancement.

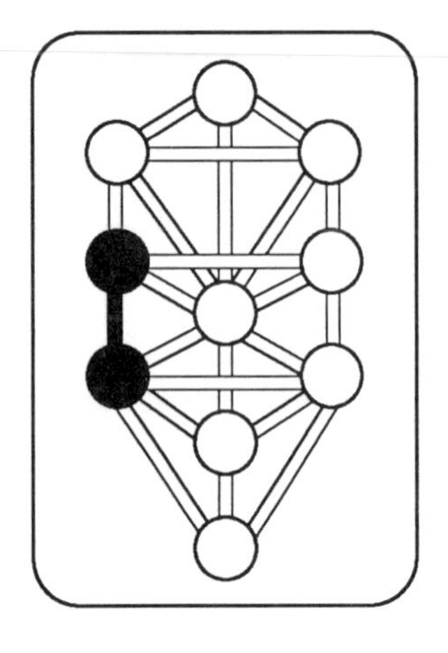

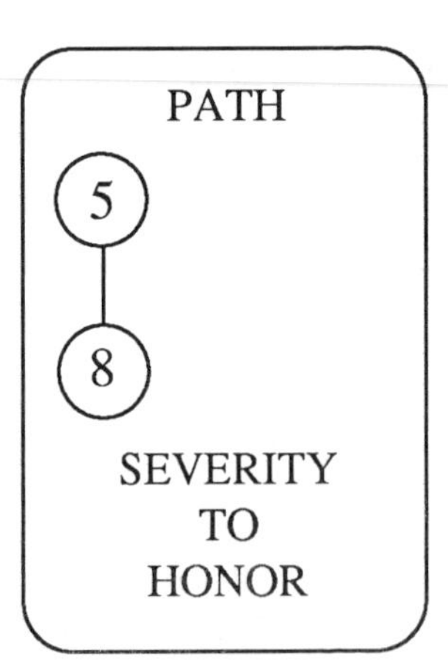

Guidance of the Path

Base your choices and decisions on something more reliable than a passing whim, mood, or emotional reaction. If your emotions are swinging you high or low, what you choose will be unbalanced and therefore transitory and unstable. Give yourself a chance to settle down, then take a look from a still point of inner peace. From that balanced perspective you can receive a more meaningful and reliable vision on which to base your actions.

Look deeper than appearances which trigger off desire. While you are in a state of <u>for</u> or <u>against</u> your perspective will be biased and your partiality unsubstantiated by the facts. Only from a neutral, unprejudiced position can you make the most reliable assessment of the facts as they are.

The more one *wants* to go forward and make a change, the longer one must wait. This is because the impatient urge to take action distorts reason and judgement. The choices one makes under this internal pressure will tend to be based on hasty, superficial observation that is all too often misleading. The typical result of taking action too soon is having to go back and do it over. Concentrate on releasing yourself from the urge to act or react; remain completely unmoved by anyone's expectations.

Surrender your freedom to a higher guiding force. Look deeper than materialistic concerns and earthly attachments. Your higher impulses are guiding you to secure and meaningful circumstances.

Examine your circumstances until you see a path which you can take which will be upheld and supported by the higher ordering forces of the universe. The only path which does this is the one which is itself in support of higher forces and conditions.

Experience Represented by the Path

This Path represents *your power to recognize what supports higher, better conditions and to release attachment to what does not.* This power rests on your ability to view yourself and your circumstances impartially, from an emotionally balanced, patient point of inner stillness. It also depends upon your willingness to surrender to your higher motives or intentions which cannot even be felt when you are reeling with emotion or desire, or ensnared by blind materialism. Conditions and individuals represented by this Path will tend to be characterized as ethereal and unusual, as well as supportive of one's higher qualities and aspirations. Experiences represented by this Path are teaching you to base your choices on clear and higher motives.

Kabbalistic Correspondences
(use for your further insight and meditation)

The Hebrew Letter associated with this Path is *Mem.* It is associated with silence and the element of water.

The Meaning of this letter is *water.* Just as water dissolves rock, that which is not based on balance and the higher motivation to give and to serve is being dissolved. As it takes time for water to penetrate its obstacle, it takes time for the deeper facts to become clearly known.

The Tarot Card associated with this Path is *Key 12, The Hanged Man.* It pictures a male hanging upside down, his right foot tied to a cross-beam which sits on two poles. His hands are tied behind his back, but his free-leg is bent, as if he was relaxed and feeling in complete control. The earth beneath his head is missing, and his eyes look straight ahead. The image represents our dependence upon higher forces, and the balanced, still point of perception which permits us to see more deeply and clearly.

The Astrological Correspondence of this Path is the planet *Neptune.* Named after the mythical *King of the Sea,* Neptune is associated with the forces of dissolution and unification; Neptune is also associated with higher, intuitive perception which penetrates the boundaries of the rational mind.

The Type of Intelligence associated with this Path is called, *Stable,* because it represents power of perception that is most reliable.

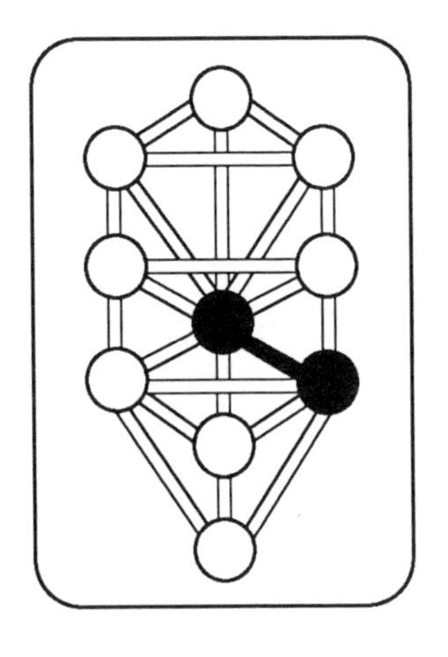

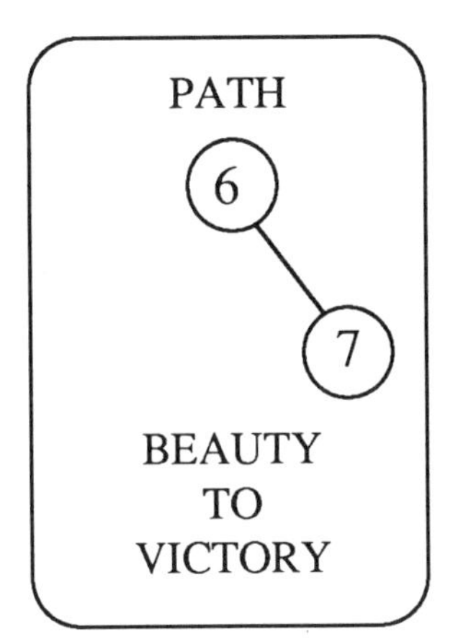

Guidance of the Path

In the end of the old is the seed of the new. Look forward to the new with joy when you have had enough of mourning for the passed. Plant the seed of your intention in the ground of the present and move on in its direction.

The onward march of life requires new ways of living. What you have achieved is behind you and the ways that brought you here may not be entirely aligned with the best way to proceed into the future. Be ready to change to seize your new opportunities before the changes in your circumstances turn against you.

Release frustrating efforts to force things. Go with the flow. Give-up your fear of giving-up control. Face what happens unafraid and you will discover that there was really nothing to fear in the first place. All fear is born of imagining something terrible. Whatever happens, you will find that you are still essentially yourself, and from that point anything is possible

Return to the ground of your *being*. Your experience of

being cannot be taken from you, nor is it diminished by any loss. Learn to trust, accept and enjoy your experience *as* an experience and you will discover that it is whole, complete and perfect as it is.

Releasing yourself from old patterns becomes necessary when they impair your capacity to take your next step into growth. When you define yourself by your previous ways of doing things you are bound to find a diminishing place, role or function in the future.

Adapt to change, even if it means leaving behind your former identity or sense of who you were. Accept the joyful attitude that you have nothing to lose and everything to gain by opening yourself to receive the new.

Holding on is holding back. No one can stop the undercurrents of change.

Experience Represented by the Path

This Path represents *your power to see through illusions of who you are and what you need.* When all that you are emotionally attached to or dependent upon is taken from you, you will find that you are still there, and that you are capable of building an entirely new life and new identity for yourself. The self that *lasts*, that is beyond *all* limiting forms of identification, is the *Real You.* Individuals and conditions represented by this Path will tend to involve, demonstrate or require intrinsic change, courage and confidence in facing the new. Experiences represented by this Path are teaching you to lose your fears and surrender attachments.

Kabbalistic Correspondences

(use for your further insight and meditation)

The Hebrew Letter associated with this Path is *Nun.* It is associated with the sense of smell, symbolic of "smelling out" subtleties.

The Meaning of this letter is *Fish* . A fish symbolizes living deeper than the surface and going with the flow. Also, as water dissolves the ground and causes change, a fish symbolizes the ability to live with and thrieve upon the forces of change.

The Tarot Card associated with this Path is *Key 13, Death.* It pictures a human skeleton with gleeful grin, suggesting joyous freedom from attachment to that which passes. Its neck is twisting around in an impossible position, symbolizing changes that require us to do what seems unnatural at first. The skeleton holds a scythe, and is surrounded by leaves, faces, hands and feet - suggesting that our sense of *identity*, ways of *handling* things are as transitory as the leaves on a tree. In the background a purple stream meets a half-view of the sun on the horizon; we can only imagine if it is rising or setting. Along the stream tall evergreens bend in the breeze toward the sun suggesting our eternal strength to bounce back and to be flexible.

The Astrological Correspondence of this Path is the constellation *Scorpio,* Latin for *Scorpion.* Astrologers associate Scorpio with the energies of sex, death and regeneration.

The Type of Intelligence associated with this Path is *Imaginative.* It teaches us that our transitory, limited sense of personal identity, dependency and attachment is imaginary and self-created.

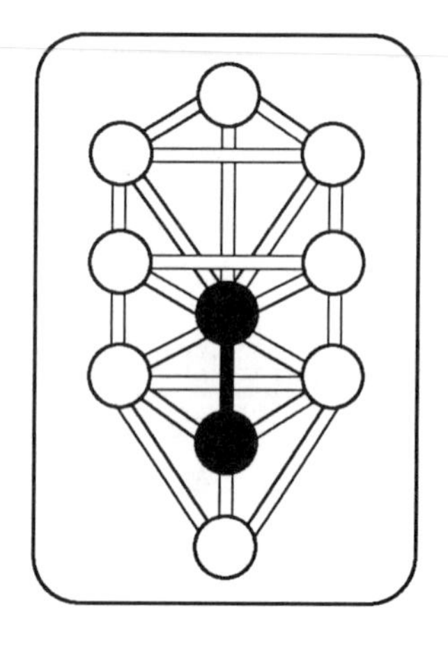

Guidance of the Path

No matter how strongly you are tempted in a given direction, it is wise to be patient, to wait until your assumptions can be tested before risking everything on them.

Life applies this same wisdom. Sooner or later in the course of seeking to change or improve yourself or your position, life will impose certain tests and trials. These serve to strengthen you, enabling you to continue moving forward. Your tests may come in the form of opportunities to satisfy a deep desire at the cost of your deeper purpose, or in the form of adversities that cut so deeply that you are strongly tempted to surrender and turn back.

There is nothing to fear in life's tests. You would be foolish to impose a test which you know is beyond the capacity of that which is tested. Life's lessons are imposed with perfect understanding of your limits, and they are designed to lead you to your next stage of progress. There is an ageless wisdom teaching which states that life will never impose upon you a test, challenge or temptation which you cannot overcome if you apply your best.

Temptation forces you to dig deeper into yourself and can cause you to question who you are. Feelings of attraction which you did not know that you were capable of can suddenly arise to sway you from your purpose and commitments. The time of trial or testing is a unique opportunity for recognizing and releasing from the deeper tendencies which would hold you back from making further advancement along your chosen course.

If you can remain calm and steady under the pressures of temptation, your higher impulses will emerge to inspire you, and deeper understanding will unfold to light your way and guide your choices.

Experience Represented by the Path

This Path represents your *power to overcome the tests and trials of life, as well as the wisdom of applying tests before jumping to conclusions.* It also represents the fact that pressure builds strength when applied in right measure. Individuals and conditions represented by this Path will tend to be tempting or attractive in the deepest way, but, to avoid self-deception, they should be patiently observed before you rely upon them. Experiences represented by this Path are teaching you to have the strength and patience to endure what is happening until you have an accurate understanding of what to do about it.

Kabbalistic Correspondences

(use for your further insight and meditation)

The Hebrew Letter associated with this Path is *Samech* (pronounced: Sah-mech). It is associated with sleep, reminding us that we are somewhat awakened by tests and trials.

The Meaning of this letter is *Prop, as in that which props up a tent.* The pole which supports a tent is symbolic of the stature which supports one's character, or the facts which supports one's assumptions - both of which are revealed by tests.

The Tarot Card associated with this Path is *Key 14, Temperance.* It pictures a great angelic being, who portrays Archangel Michael. The angel stands with his right foot in a pool of water while his left foot leans on the grassy bank; he seems to be lifting and lowering himself simultaneously, symbolizing growth through pressure. At the same time he holds a flaming torch in his left hand over the head of an eagle, and he pours a stream of water onto the head of a lion from a pitcher he holds in his right. In the background a brilliant crown hovers above a path that cuts between two mountains of roughly equal height. Above the angel is a rainbow, symbol of promise and protection. The image portrays growth or advancement through baalaance.

The Astrological Correspondence of this Path is the constellation of *Sagittarius,* which is Latin for *archer.* Astrologers associate Sagittarius with optimism, which helps us to overcome life's challenges; and also with the urge to grow and expand which brings those tests and challenges upon us.

The Type of Intelligence associated with this Path is called, *The Intelligence of Trial and Probation* , for it represents the wisdom of testing oneself, individuals, circumstances and ideas before depending too heavily upon them.

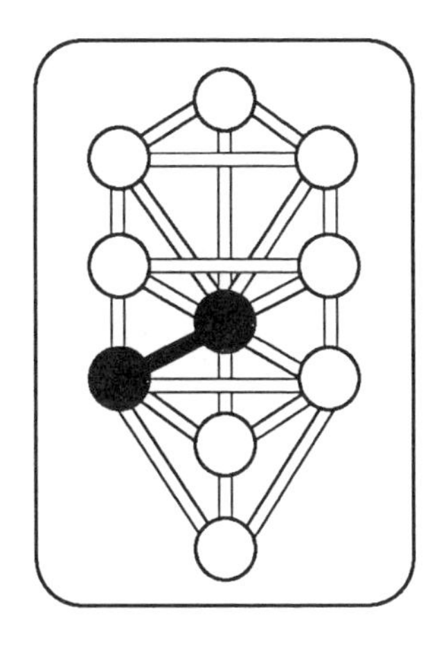

Guidance of the Path

Imagining what can go wrong induces fear. But that fear is based on imagination; it is an emotional reaction to a vision of being dominated by terrible possibilities. To the extent that you believe in limiting possibilities you limit and bring out the worst in yourself.

See through the illusions of fear. The dominance of evil, injustice or cruelty is illusory. There is good in everything. Look for the light and you will find it.

Imagination can create a belief in a reality that does not exist. That which stimulates desire following superficial observation promises pleasure in the nature of its *appearance*. However, sensual desire alone is not an adequate guide to happiness, security and peace. Doing something for money is not necessarily wise either. Materialistic interests only represent a portion of your need and responsibility. What you have to do *for* the money is also important. Anything that requires you to demean or to deceive others or yourself is already too expensive.

Take responsibility for your behavior and you will find that you can change that behavior. Identify the weaknesses in yourself which bring you down and hold you back and concentrate on freeing yourself from them. As long as you regard others or external circumstances as the cause of what you do, you give that power to them.

It is up to *you* to free yourself from oppression. It is one thing to be responsible and another to overtax yourself to the point that your labor loses its meaning and your life has lost its joy. Dedication to even the highest ideals is demoralizing when we drive ourselves or others too hard. The insistence on perfection, past a certain point, becomes counter-productive. Have faith in the path of honor, peace, balance and love.

Experience Represented by the Path

This Path represents *your power to see through appearances, to overcome temptation, and to respect the spark of divinity, or limitless potential, in yourself and others.* The foundation of this Power is in *notforcing*. Forcing strengthens the lower as faith supports the higher. Individuals and conditions represented by this Path will tend to be characterized by an opportunity to see through illusion and to break the dominance of fear. Experiences represented by this Path are teaching you to avoid choices that lead to self-degradation and to release yourself from the burden of fear and oppressiveness.

Kabbalistic Correspondences
(use for your further insight and meditation)

The Hebrew Letter associated with this Path is *Ayin* . It is said to predominate in anger.

The Meaning of this letter is Eye. It reminds us to read the heart by looking in the eye.

The Tarot Card associated with this Path is *Key 15, The Devil.* It pictures a monstrous creature perched on a narrow, rectangular pedestal which appears top-heavy and unstable. He has the horns and head of a goat, the wings of a bat, the torso and arms of a man, and the legs and claws of an eagle. Chained to the pedestal stands a nude male and female, with horns on their heads, hooves for feet and tails. The female seems to be offering her body for pleasure, but behind her back she drops a handful of ashes, seemingly of her last victim. The male seems to be offering an open hand, but he's hiding something behind his back. The chains around their necks are apparently loose enough for them to free themselves at will. The image portrays our Power to free ourselves from our lower impulses, which rule us when we depend on what we fear.

The Astrological Correspondence of this Path is the constellation, *Capricorn,* which is Latin for, *he-goat.* Capricorn is associated with personal ambition, the sense of responsibility and the drive to rule, dominate or control.

The Type of Intelligence associated with this Path is called, *Renewing and Renovative,* because when we recognize how we are oppressing and frightening *ourselves* we have found the key to our liberation.

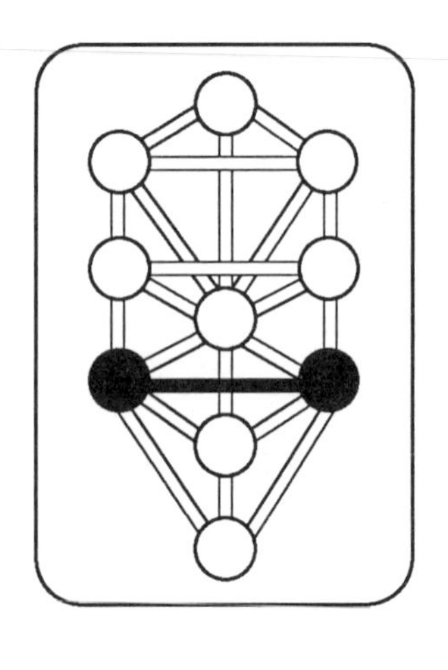

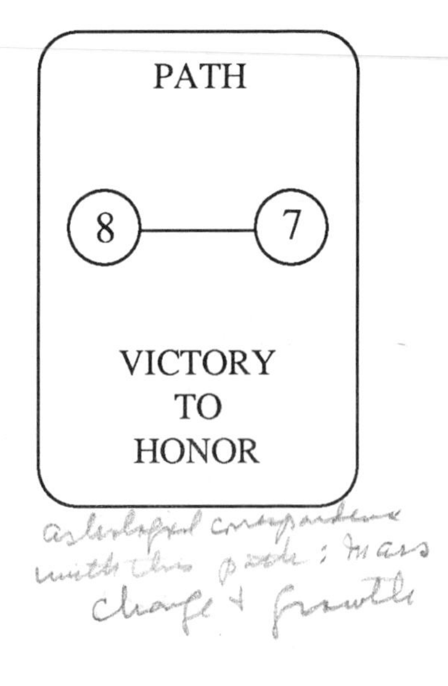

Guidance of the Path

Accept the fallibility of human creations, as well as the fallibility of the ideas and concepts of human understanding. Whatever you conceive a thing to be, it will prove to be quite different before long. Eventually, the limitations inherent in any human design make it untenable and it then must be revised or discarded. It is therefore wise not to place too much importance on your beliefs, opinions and desires. What seems just "right" today will eventually seem just as "wrong"; and vice versa.

Theories, ideas and opinions are temporary at best, and even then they can only point to a fraction of the truth. Utilize them but avoid becoming stuck in them.

Disruption is a natural fact of life. Sooner or later a force will enter any condition as a chaotic influence. Accept it as a natural phenomenon although it may shake you to the bone. Do not question yourself and think that you must have made a wrong decision because you suddenly find yourself dissatisfied. Any choice you make will eventually encounter a cycle of disorder.

Have the humility to be flexible with regard to the standards you set for yourself and others. There is more to each individual than can be understood. Your standards represent the limitations of your understanding of what would be best, of what "should" happen. And yet, just because things do not occur as you expect, that does not mean that the way they are happening is inferior. You do not *know* what you can only *believe*.

Upon leaving your expectations behind, you may find yourself disoriented and uncertain. Things may seem so up in the air that you cannot even formulate an opinion, nor have any idea of what to do. Learn how to live without expectations.

Experience Represented by the Path

This Path represents *your power to move beyond your ideas and expectations*. All theories, assumptions and speculations are at best like drops from the ocean of truth. Your concepts and opinions, and the schemes you base upon them, are limited, transitory and imperfect. It is therefore wise not to place too much value or importance on your point of view, or anyone else's for that matter. The unforeseen, overlooked, unpredicted, unincluded sooner or later enters to upset the status quo. Individuals and conditions represented by this Path will tend to involve a departure from established trends and destabilization of existing patterns. Experiences represented by this Path are teaching you how to live beyond your expectations.

Kabbalistic Correspondences

(use for your further insight and meditation)

The Hebrew Letter associated with this Path is *Pe* (pronounced: Peh). It is associated with power.

The Meaning of this letter is *Mouth* as an organ of speech. Along this path, it is a reminder that whatever one can say about a fact cannot cover all that there is to know about it.

The Tarot Card associated with this Path is *Key 16, The Tower*. It pictures a tower being struck by a lightening bolt. The bolt exhibits a zigzag pattern that follows the pattern of the Tree of Life along the sequence of its Spheres. It is emerging from the Sun in the upper right-hand corner of the image. The bolt hits the top of the tower, toppling its huge crown that made the tower top-heavy. Flames are shooting out from the windows of the tower and two human beings soar down, head-first through the air. The image represents the inevitable encounter with the upset of every human plan, concept and design.

The Astrological Correspondence of this Path is the planet *Mars*. Astrologers associate Mars with conflict and change.

The Type of Intelligence associated with this Path is called, *Exciting*, for this Path represents the motions and commotions of change and growth.

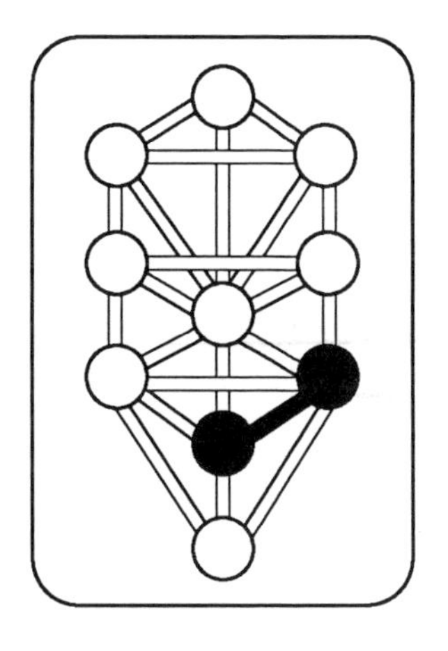

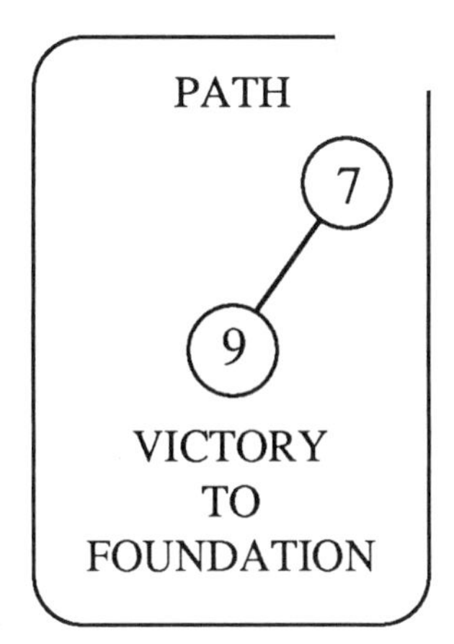

Guidance of the Path

To receive the deeper flash of knowing, free your mind of distracting interests and concerns, as well as all superficial ideas and opinions pertaining to your issue. Consider the past to see what you can learn from it, but do not project the past onto the present. The here-now is always new, and the possibilities of what will be are different than they were before. Contemplate the future as well. Observe the current trends to make intelligent predictions of what is likely to occur. Intuition is the illuminating point where the past, present and future meet.

When an immediate solution does not occur, individuals are tempted to believe that there is no answer to receive. However, the solution to no solution is to look more deeply. There is a way to advance toward your goal and achieve your objective. If it defies the capacities of your rational mind, it is still within the scope of your intuition to recognize. Examine your thoughts, feelings, mood and attitude patiently and persistently to uncover any ways that you are resisting or interfering with the clear, deeper knowing you seek. If your mind is filled with other matters, or if you are believing that you will not, do not, or cannot know the answer, you are pushing it out of the space of your awareness and effectively keeping it hidden from yourself.

While it is intelligent to consider the likely possibilities, do not presume that you know what is going to happen when you really do not. One of the great obstacles to receiving a clear answer is *expectations*. If you *expect* to hear a certain answer to your question you may deafen yourself to the actual response that you receive, and imagine that you heard what you were ready to hear. Examine yourself carefully to uncover any expectations that could be interfering with your receptivity. Let go of these when you notice them, and remain open and receptive to the inner flash of knowing.

Experience Represented by the Path

This Path represents *your power to receive solutions for any problem in life.* That power is meditation. Superficial thinking, expectations and a negative attitude make problems seem impossible to solve. Meditate by focusing on your issue with openness to the answer; this literally draws the inner flash of reliable knowing to you, the way a baited hook draws a fish from the water's depths. Conditions and individuals represented by this Path will tend to be characterized by sudden flashes of inspired vision that points the way. The experience represented by this Path is teaching you to meditate patiently until you receive the answers that you need.

Kabbalistic Correspondences
(use for your further insight and meditation)

The Hebrew Letter associated with this Path is *Tzaddi* (pronounced: T-zah-dee). It is associated with the sense of taste, which occurs as food is dissolved upon the tongue.

The Meaning of this letter is *fishhook.* As a fishhook descends beneath the surface to draw out a fish, so does the mind draw out that which is hidden through the act of meditation.

The Tarot Card associated with this Path is *Key 17, The Star*. It pictures a young woman in the nude, symbolizing awareness of the inner self. She is kneeling over a pool of water, symbol of the mind. She holds two jugs, one in each hand, symbolizing the two modes of consciousness: receptive and transmittive. From one she pours water back into the pool, cleansing her receptive consciousness; from the other she pours water onto the grass-covered ground, symbolizing the application of clear thinking to life. Above the pool is a great star, symbol of the guiding light she seeks. The image symbolizes the cleansing of the mind and its descent into the depths to receive a great flash of insight that can be applied to life.

The Astrological Correspondence of this Path is the constellation, *Aquarius,* which is Latin for, *water bearer*. Aquarius is associated with the mind's capacity to experience deep, unexpected flashes of intuitive knowing.

The Type of Intelligence associated with this Path is called *Natural* , because it represents the natural process for giving birth to solutions.

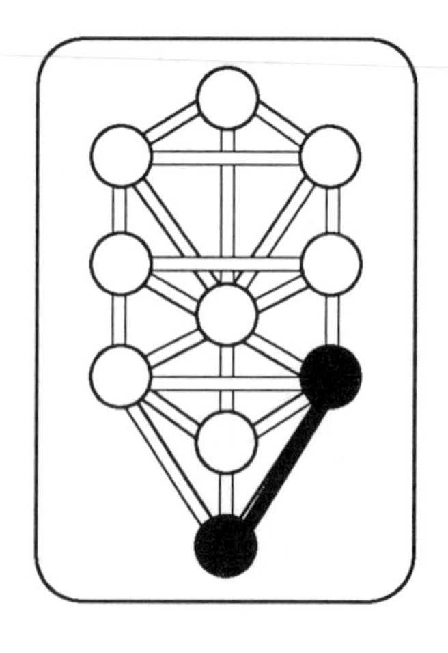

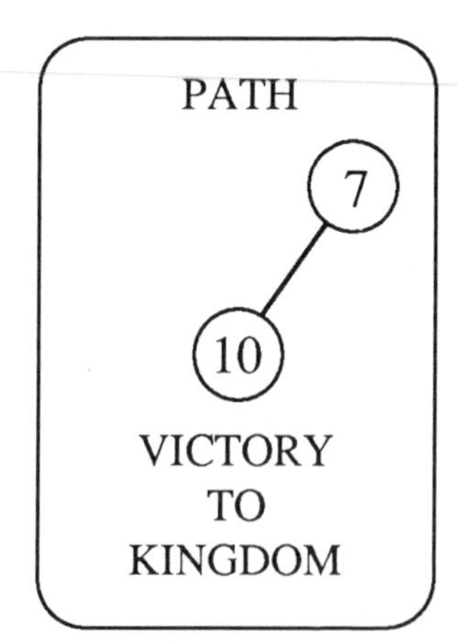

Guidance of the Path

Take note of your primitive, instinctive impulses. Observe your responses even at this most basic level in order to obtain an honest, balanced view of how you feel and what you need to do. These are as much a part of your total self-consciousness as your more refined, intellectual nature.

There is a certain wisdom in the instinctive drives. Instinctive intelligence guided the building of your physical organism, and continues to keep it going without your thought, awareness or control. The guiding purpose behind the instincts is the same as that which is behind your loftiest pursuits: the continuing evolution of your consciousness. This purpose is the aim of life itself, the reason for the cosmos and the meaning behind every experience. As long as your aim is consistent with this cosmic endeavor, your path will lead toward accomplishment.

Thinking can confuse as well as clarify. Wondering and guessing often stirs up doubt of what is true. Return to the guidance of your most basic instincts. Take heed of the promptings in your physical body. They are a kind of compass, guiding you toward the light.

Build your understanding from the ground up. Follow your sense of what *feels* most consistent in your body. All conflict is expressed through feelings of physical blockage.

Your physical body is a representation of your consciousness. Look deeper than ideas, deeper than emotion, deeper than desire. If you can, contact your *urge to grow*, for that is the intrinsic guide. However, if you cannot sense this, *simply listen to your body*. If something gives you a sense of physical strength, well-being and congruence, it is in all likelihood leading you in the right direction.

Experience Represented by the Path

This Path represents *your power to attune to higher consciousness through your physical body*. Your body is a kind of consciousness-attunement device, a sort of *dowsing rod*, which can extend your awareness into the superconscious realms. Pay attention to its subtle promptings and your sensitivity to its inner directive will awaken. Individuals and conditions represented by this Path are characterized by physical well-being and movement toward improved conditions. Experiences represented by this Path are teaching you to pay attention to your feelings and to trust your deepest urge.

Kabbalistic Correspondences

(use for your further insight and meditation)

The Hebrew Letter associated with this Path is *Qoph* (pronounced: Koff). It is associated with laughter.

The Meaning of this letter is *Back of the head*. This part of the head houses the region of the brain which governs the instinctive functions of the body.

The Tarot Card associated with this Path is *Key 18, The Moon.* It pictures a pool encircled by small stones and a few dark, primitive weeds growing through the narrow spaces between them. A lobster is emerging from the pool and enters upon a path which travels endlessly before it, over grassy hills and dales along a plane of gradual ascent. Just ahead of the lobster a wolf is baying at the moon above. Opposite the wolf is a barking dog. Up ahead are two man-made gun-towers on opposite sides of the path. The moon above is encircled by the sun just behind it. The face of the moon is looking down at the scene below. The image represents the evolutionary stages in each of us, from the mineral kingdom to the primordial pool, to the dark weeds, the grass, wild animal, domesticated animal and to the violent barbarism of humankind. The moon in the sun represents the personality aligned with the Spiritual Sun, symbolizing the highest level of human evolution: the stage known as Enlightenment.

The Astrological Correspondence of this Path is the constellation *Pisces,* Latin for *fishes*. Pisces is the last sign of the Zodiac and is associated with unity, sympathy and synthesis of all of the previous stages.

The Type of Intelligence associated with this Path is called *Corporeal*, for it represents the instinctive intelligence demonstrated by living, physical organisms.

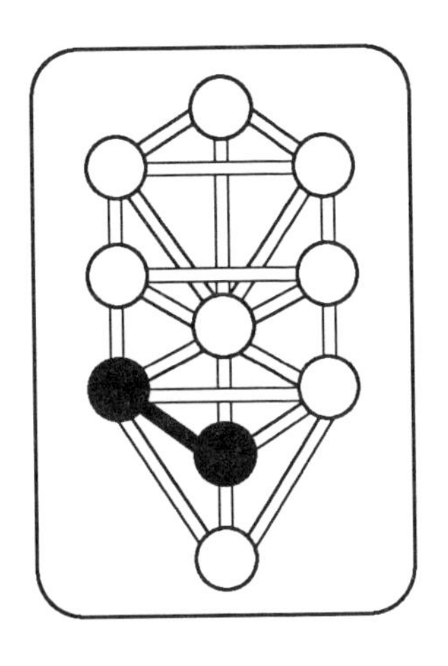

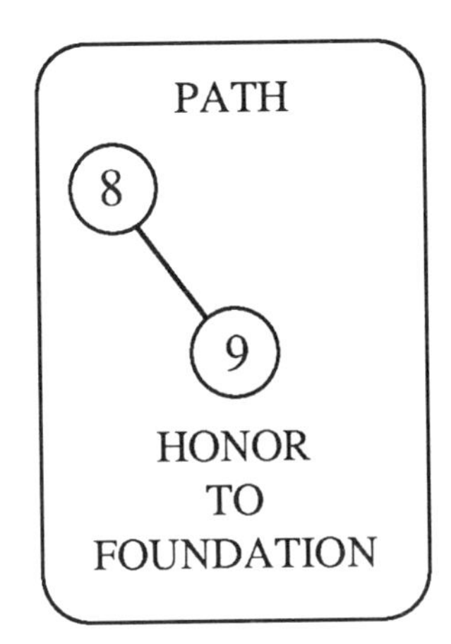

Guidance of the Path

Take responsibility for raising yourself. What you do gives birth to who you are. The self you are expressing is the self you are creating.

You have the right to sing and dance with joy in the sun. Be as a child: simple, innocent and free.

The adequate response to what you are going through will comc naturally to you if you let it. It will bloom like a flower. Forcing yourself to respond in a way that seems unnatural or dishonest interferes with this process. You are naturally drawn along the path that will bring harmony and balance into your life. It is your real, inner nature to be a giving source of love, life and light. Look within and be receptive to your deeper sense of self.

In your heart exists a sense of yourself in a pure, joyful, loving state. Your innermost intentions are doubtlessly beyond reproach. If only you could express this *Golden Child,* if only you could be your Higher Self! How long will you continue to hold-back, to force artificial, unnatural restraints on your self? Those old patterns harden like a shell. But it is time for the love, life and light within to come out and live to its full potential. Give your self to the one you long in your heart to be.

Now is your opportunity to begin. Discard old, automatic patterns of action and reaction and be renewed. It is never too late to make the right decision. Wherever you are, however you may have done things in the past, give your more pure, inner nature a chance run things in the present.

Your higher nature is like a child, desiring only to nurture and be nurtured. Go deeper than your hard and crusty shell and follow the guidance of the child in your heart. Respect your inner child and give birth to your higher potential.

Experience Represented by the Path

This Path represents *your power to regenerate.* It is your power to nurture, support and bring out the higher potential in yourself and others, and to create new, improved conditions from failing or less adequate conditions of the past. This is accomplished as you follow the guidance of your loving nature and concentrate on doing what you can in the present for the future, not distracted by what may or may not have happened in the past. Conditions and individuals represented by this Path will tend to seem easy to deal with, natural and full of hope. Experiences represented by this Path are teaching you to base your choices on what is, rather than on what was, and to be guided in your self expression by the self you want to be.

Kabbalistic Correspondences

(use for your further insight and meditation)

The Hebrew Letter associated with this Path is *Resh.* It is associated with peace, the state your higher nature craves.

The Meaning of this letter is *Front of the head, or Face.* Your face is a symbol of your outward expression; when this matches your innermost feelings and intent, your Higher Self is truly born.

The Tarot Card associated with this Path is *Key 19, The Sun.* It pictures two naked children, a boy and a girl, dancing hand-in-hand inside a circle beneath a giant, friendly sun. Behind them is a wall behind which five huge sunflowers are contained. The circle and wall represent the restraints or boundaries of self-containment, reminding us that giving expression to our higher potential in our current circumstances requires that we resist the urge to act or react under the influence of our past habits. Their nudity represents release, disclosure or revelation of that which is within. The children themselves represent a new stage or level of expression of the Higher Self. The Sun represents the energy of life that empowers that expression. As a whole the image portrays the process of re-creation or regeneration.

The Astrological Correspondence of this Path is the *Sun.* Astrologers associate its placement with the expression of your true, basic nature, as well as with your energy-source of life and creativity.

The Type of Intelligence associated with this Path is *Collective* because each moment offers an opportunity to contribute to the unfoldment of a new, higher condition by adding to the collection of events.

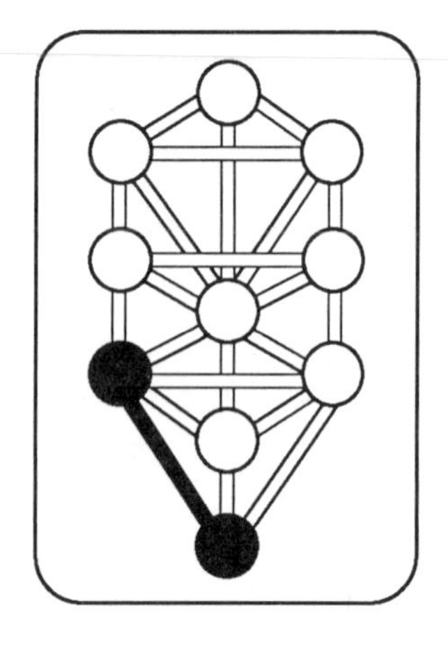

Guidance of the Path

Be grateful for what you have achieved and received so far. Permit yourself to feel appreciation for the progress you have made. This impresses your subconscious with a clear signal of your intent, releasing your creative forces to continue working in that direction. Expressing your gratitude and appreciation to others lets them know what you value, so they will have a clearer sense as to how they can serve, please or assist you. However, in life and in your relationships, do not insist on receiving only what you think you want. Accept the fact that a worthwhile purpose is being served by whatever happens.

If you look for the higher value in an event, situation or individual's activities you can discover it. Refuse to limit your perspective to hasty opinions based on superficial examination of the the facts. Seek out the inner meaning which is there.

Sometimes, receiving exactly what you want *least* turns

out to be the very thing that is best for you. Life is filled with disappointments until we realize that our expectations are not rooted in the reality of who we are, what is truly going on, and what we need. Identify the trends toward improvement that are present all the time and fix your approval onto these. On the surface things seem to alternate between good times and bad; but underneath there is perpetual movement toward growth and improvement.

Wake-up to the inner meaning of what you are going through and you will realize that you have nothing to pity yourself for and nothing to fear. Even suffering has a purpose; it teaches us to release our attachment to conditions that pass, and to seek a deeper level of understanding that will bring us to a place of more lasting peace.

Experience Represented by the Path

This Path represents *your power to recognize the perpetual motions of the cosmos*. This enables one to recognize what to be grateful for in life. Individuals and conditions represented by this Path will tend to benefit from endings and disappointments. Experiences represented by this Path are teaching you to be forever hopeful.

Kabbalistic Correspondences

(use for your further insight and meditation)

The Hebrew Letter associated with this Path is *Shin*. It is associated with *fire which carries water*. Fire or heat on water produces steam, which *carries water upward*. Water is a symbol of knowledge or the substance of consciousness; fire represents the will to raise your knowledge or understanding to a higher plane.

The Meaning of this letter is *Tooth.* A tooth penetrates the surface flesh of that which is eaten. This Path represents the Power of your consciousness to penetrate the superficial and the transitory to enter the eternal realms.

The Tarot Card associated with this Path is *Key 20, Judgement.* It pictures three individuals: a man, a woman, and a child. They are nude, to suggest purity, openness and revelation. Each rises out of their own individual coffin. The coffins of the adults are rectangular, and the coffin of the child which stands between them is square. They are filled with darkness and float upon the water. In the background are mountains of snow, suggesting the purity of higher spititual planes. Above them, Archangel Gabriel blows his horn of awakening, the horn which calls us to eternal life. The two adults look up with with gratitude and reverence. The child's back is turned toward us while he gives all of his attention to the angel, and receives with open arms the full force of the blowing horn. Looking more closely at the position of the arms of the people we see that they seem to spell: L V X, which is Latin for *Light.* The image represents the awakening of consciousness to the permanent and eternal.

The Astrological Correspondence of this Path is the planet *Pluto.* Astrologers associate Pluto with the power to rise above that which passes and to go deeper than the surface.

The Type of Intelligence associated with this Path is called *Perpetual,* because it represents the eternal in time.

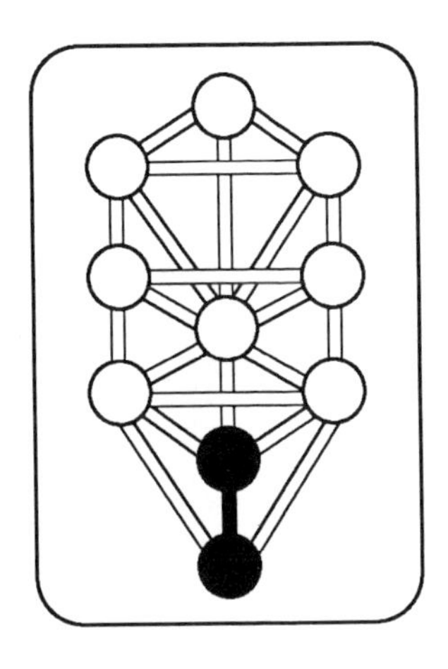

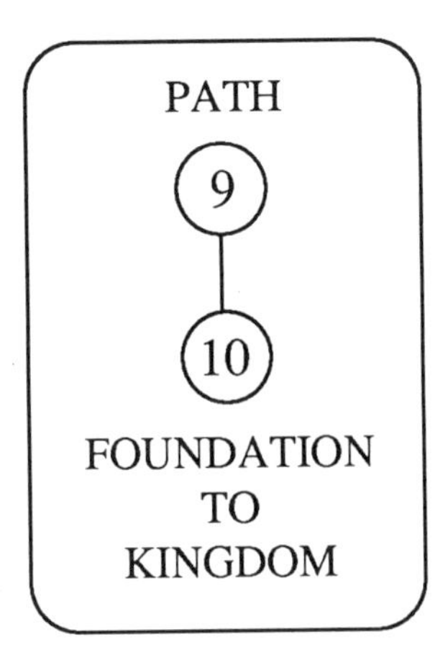

Guidance of the Path

When the fruit is ripe it lends itself to easy plucking. If you must force the fruit from the vine, it is not ripe yet. Nature offers resistance as a protection. Unripe fruit sickens its consumer. Follow the principle of ripeness in your endeavors. Regard resistance to your efforts as a sign that things are as yet at a premature stage. Give them time to ripen, when it will be easier to move forward and the results of doing so will be sweeter.

The universe offers you the fruits of your labor when the outcome you intend is in line with *its* greater purpose. What you can accomplish, and what you have achieved thus far, is consistent with the cosmic aim. Although you may take personal pleasure in your rewards, acknowledge that the rest of the universe had to cooperate to make this possible. Do not presume that it was an accident or luck which brought you to this place. Something much larger is going on which this is but a minute part of. Consider the deeper significance of what is happening, and align yourself with *that.* The fact that you are pleased by the results you have achieved is the only *accident,* if you want to call it that. Enjoy the special moment of coincidence, when your personal interests and the interests of the cosmos seem to be a perfect *match.*

Recognize the authority of your will and skill. Bringing about the outcome you have intended and worked for is indeed a great feat. You have shaped your own destiny through the application of your will and skill. What you are experiencing is a product of the handiwork you have been a channel for. Examine what you have brought about to discover how to do things better in the future.

Reap the fruits of your labor and realize the fulfillment of your intention. There is no escape from what you have set into motion. It is now your task to make the best of it.

Experience Represented by the Path

This Path represents *your power to be guided by the Cosmic Will.* It represents your ability to sense what *wants* to happen, and lend the forces of your skill and will toward bringing it about. This stage of mastery is called, *Cosmic Co-Creator.* Individuals and conditions represented by this Path will tend to be characterized by mastery and reciprocity. Experiences represented by this Path are teaching you to recognize, trust and cooperate with the undercurrent of the Cosmic Will.

Kabbalistic Correspondences

(use for your further insight and meditation)

The Hebrew Letter associated with this Path is *Tav.* It is associated with grace.

The Meaning of this letter is *Mark, Signature.* When you place your mark or sign your name to something, you take responsibility for the consequences. In the same way, you are responsible for the mark you leave, the impression you make, in life.

The Tarot Card associated with this Path is *Key 21, The World.* It pictures an androgynous being dancing in the sky. Refer back to the image of Key 0, associated with Path 1-2. If we have been watching the same being throughout the images of Tarot, it would suggest that the Fool was not so foolish, because his leap of faith did not lead to a fall. The image of Key 21 is named the world to suggest that the purpose of our descent into earthly life is to ultimately rise above it. The andgrogyne is surrounded by a wreathe of ultimate Victory. His/her left leg is bent behind the right, indicating ease, grace and the sense of being in control. The being holds a spiral in each hand, representing mastery of positive (outflowing) and negative (indrawing) force and skill. Outside the wreathe, at the four corners of the image, are the same heads we saw in Key 10 along Path 4-7. In this image they represent the Cosmic Will directing events. The image as a whole represents the result or reward of cooperating with the Cosmic Will.

The Astrological Correspondence of this Path is the planet Saturn. Astrologers associate Saturn with administration skills.

The Type of Intelligence associated with this Path is called *Administrative,* because this Path represents mastery in the administration of your power to direct your life.

"There is neither light nor darkness in it, but the souls devoted to the inner flame, as from behind a wall, discern the light which it sends forth and which illumines the supreme heaven, a light never ceasing, a light not to be known or grasped."

from: The Zohar

Additional Sources

The following sources have been greatly supportive in my consciousness-work, and I recommend them to you as keys to deeper understanding and the wisdom of Kabbalah:

The School of the Natural Order

Offering the written and taped works of Vitvan, whose work provides a solid grounding in the ageless wisdom from a contemporary, intellectual perspective. For more information write:

The School of the Natural Order
Box 578
Baker, Nevada 89311

Diamond Fire

A quarterly publication founded and edited by Joseph Polansky. It is dedicated to the esoteric wisdom tradition. For more information write to:

Malchitsedek Productions
3704 Lyme Avenue
Brooklyn, New York 11224

MetaBusiness Institute

Founded by Greg Nielsen, it offers live programs and publications dedicated to supporting an international business environment that is in harmony with the energy needs of the individual. For more information write to:

MetaBusiness Institute
316 California Avenue #210
Reno, Nevada 89509

The Organics Wisdom Library

Established and supervised by Nancy Dahlberg, offering the writings and taped lectures of my first Wisdom Teacher, Isidore Friedman. For further information write to:

The Organics Wisdom Library
3735 Oceanic Avenue
Brooklyn, New York 11224

Bob Lancer is the author of several books on Ageless Wisdom, and the creator of The Kabbalah Cards. He has degrees in English and Education, with Graduate level training in Counseling Psychology and Education. Following his graduation from Long Island University in 1974 at the age of 22, he studied Organics with Isidore Friedman, who introduced him to the Esoteric Wisdom Tradition, and initiated him into the path to higher consciousness. Since 1980 he has been presenting consultations and classes to groups and individuals aimed at clarifying the deeper spiritual teachings and assisting individuals in the application of those teachings to their lives. He currently lives in Marietta, Georgia with his wife Karmelah, a spiritually based psychotherapist and intuitive reader. Accompanying them on their path are their two dogs, Arjuna and Sushumna who are taking very good care of them.

1 Aleph – divine name

2 Chokmah – Wisdom – archangel

Path

(3) – (2)

Wisdom

to

Understanding